GOD'S *ETERNAL*
Scheme of Redemption
Our Plan of Salvation from the Bondage of Sin

WEEKLY READING SCHEDULE		CONTRIBUTORS
SIN AND THE PROMISED SEED OF THE WOMAN	WEEK 1:	Cheryle & Donny Bryan
INSTITUTION OF THE SACRIFICE FOR SIN	WEEK 2:	B. J. & Don Lockey
ABRAHAM AND THE COVENANT OF CIRCUMCISION	WEEK 3:	Michael Willis
MOSES AND THE COVENANT OF LAW	WEEK 4:	Mike Paine
PASSOVER AND DELIVERY FROM SLAVERY	WEEK 5:	Richard Hamlen
TYPES AND SHADOWS, THEN AND NOW	WEEK 6:	Marilyn & John King
SACRED EXAMPLES OF HOLINESS	WEEK 7:	John Hunt
DELIVERANCE FROM JOSHUA TO JESUS	WEEK 8:	Debbie Paine
OUR REDEEMER INTRODUCED	WEEK 9:	Carrie Seat
CHRIST'S NATURE, CHARACTER AND PERSONALITY	WEEK 10:	Jerry Deloach
WHY THE WORD BECAME FLESH	WEEK 11:	Don Seat
THE HOLY SPIRIT IN REDEMPTION	WEEK 12:	Byron Brown
PROPHETS AND APOSTLES IN THE REDEMPTION PLAN	WEEK 13:	Myra Anderson
THE REDEMPTIVE PROCESS "IN CHRIST"	WEEK 14:	Homer Anderson
THE CHURCH: FELLOWSHIP OF THE SAVED	WEEK 15:	Janet Brown
REDEMPTIVE LEADERSHIP "IN CHRIST"	WEEK 16:	Leon Weeks
PREACHING THE MESSAGE OF REDEMPTION	WEEK 17:	Kenny Holton
WORSHIP PRAISE TO OUR REDEEMER	WEEK 18:	G. R. Holton
THE LORD'S DAY AND GIVING	WEEK 19:	Ruth Harrison
LORD'S SUPPER: REMEMBERING OUR REDEEMER	WEEK 20:	Carol McLeod
CONDITIONS OF CHURCH MEMBERSHIP	WEEK 21:	Marie Weeks
SERVING THE WORLD	WEEK 22:	Kevin Boyd
GOD'S LOVE REFLECTED IN HIS DISCIPLES	WEEK 23:	Francine Coppage
THE PEACE THAT PASSES UNDERSTANDING	WEEK 24:	Toni Webb
THE CHURCHES OF CHRIST	WEEK 25:	John Klimko
CONFIDENT IN "I BELIEVE…"	WEEK 26:	Ronnie West
BONUS: FORTUNES AND DESTINY OF THE REDEEMED	WEEK 27:	G. R. Holton

7th BIBLE READING MARATHON

SPONSORED AND DEVELOPED BY THE CENTRAL AVENUE CHURCH OF CHRIST

304 EAST CENTRAL AVENUE - VALDOSTA, GEORGIA
PHONE: (229) 242-6115 <central@cacoc.com> Website: www.cacoc.com

7th Bible Reading Marathon

God's *Eternal* Scheme of Redemption

Our Plan of Salvation from the Bondage of Sin
A 27-week Topical Bible Reading Schedule

The Bible Reading Marathon is designed as a tool to encourage Bible reading.	*General Editor:* **G. R. Holton**
We believe the Bible is the inerrant, inspired Word of God.	*Your Stories...:* **Toni Ellen Webb**
We believe reading and studying the Bible builds faith in God.	*Copy Reviewers:* **Debbie Paine**
We believe the life of a Christian is vibrant faith in action.	**Marie Weeks** **Kevin Boyd**
We believe faithful Christians make reading the Bible a daily habit.	*Plus* **Twenty-six Scripture Text Compilers** Contact: grholton@yahoo.com

©Growing Panes

Published by
Growing Panes, Inc.
3543 Raintree Drive
Valdosta, Georgia 31601

7TH BIBLE READING MARATHON

GOD'S *ETERNAL* SCHEME OF REDEMPTION

TABLE OF CONTENTS

7TH BIBLE READING MARATHON

DEDICATION

HOMER ANDERSON	RUTH HARRISON	JOHN MANFRA
MYRA ANDERSON	KENNY HOLTON	CAROL MCLEOD
KEVIN BOYD	G. R. HOLTON	DEBBIE PAINE
BYRON BROWN	JOHN HUNT	MIKE PAINE
JANET BROWN	BRYAN JARVIS	CARRIE SEAT
CHERYLE BRYAN	LARRY JONAS	DON SEAT
DONNY BRYAN	MARILYN KING	TONI WEBB
FRANCINE COPPAGE	JOHN KING	MARIE WEEKS
GLENN COPELAND	JOHN KLIMKO	LEON WEEKS
JERRY DELOACH	AL LITTLE	RONNIE WEST
O'NEAL GRANT	B. J. LOCKEY	MICHAEL WILLIS
RICHARD HAMLEN	DON LOCKEY	
RACHEL HAYES	BILL MALONE	

The *7th Bible Reading Marathon* is hereby dedicated to the men and women who have compiled the Scriptures for all seven Marathons. Most of them have been involved from the beginning. Some have been unable to continue due to various reasons. Each one has dedicated hours in research, editing and review. Some reported they spent more than ten hours on their week. Based on that, those who have been with us for all BRMs (except #1) have invested approximately sixty or seventy hours. Nearly 2000 hours have been dedicated to this work by the compilers and editors. These are all mature, serious students of the Bible. Many are Bible class teachers. Their lives reflect both the spirit and character of Christ.

In addition to the Marathon compilers, each compiler asked two other individuals to review their work and read the passages prior to publication. Thus, 78 Christians were involved in the preparation and review of each of the BRMs.

History of the Bible Reading Marathon

The first *Bible Reading Marathon* was conducted at Central Avenue in fall of 2012 and spring of 2013. The first fifteen weeks were devoted to "training" with an increasing number of Scriptures each week. For the remaining twelve weeks, a chronological reading of the entire New Testament was scheduled.

Seventy percent (70%) of the congregation signed up for the program. One hundred fifty-nine (159) finished the race at the end of twenty-six weeks.

The expressed purpose of the BRM was to "encourage Christians to develop the *habit* of regularly reading their Bibles." "Habit" is the key word in the program based on *The Power of Habit* by Charles Duhigg (Random House, New York, NY, 2012). The goal was to make regular Bible reading as common and routine as brushing your teeth!

According to Duhigg, habit formation is the process by which a behavior, through regular repetition, becomes automatic or habitual. Strong habits become almost compulsory. As the habit is forming, it can be analyzed in three parts: the **cue**, the **behavior** and the **reward**. The *cue* is the thing that causes your habit to come about, the trigger to your habitual behavior. This could be anything that your mind associates with that habit, and you will automatically let a habit come to the surface. The *behavior* is the actual habit that you are exhibiting and the *reward*, a positive feeling, therefore continues the "habit loop." A habit may initially be triggered by a goal, but over time that goal becomes less necessary and the habit becomes more automatic.

Thus, based on Duhigg's three-part *"habit formation"* formula, the **Bible Reading Marathon** is :

A. *The Cues,* or triggers in the BRM schedule includes posted scriptures, a time-table for reading, and beginning and ending cycles.

B. *The Routine,* or the behavior patterns that must become repetitive over time is simply the completed task of completing the Bible reading schedules on a regular basis.

C. *The Rewards,* or the positive, good feeling you experience for completing the behavior and completing the course. In addition, runners in the Bible Reading Marathon enjoy the knowledge of being blessed by pleasing God.

The Bible Reading Marathon is just *a tool* to help you develop the habit of regularly reading your Bible! Strong "good" habits are just as hard to break as bad habits. Regular Bible reading is a good habit.

1st BRM: Chronological Bible Readings

The first BRM was compiled by the editor to read the Bible in a chronological way. It was just a typical reading schedule.

After the first year, a dedicated group of serious Bible students, many of whom are teachers of adult Bible classes, was assembled to research and compile the Scripture passages for topical readings around a common theme. The style changed to a "three-lane" race format.

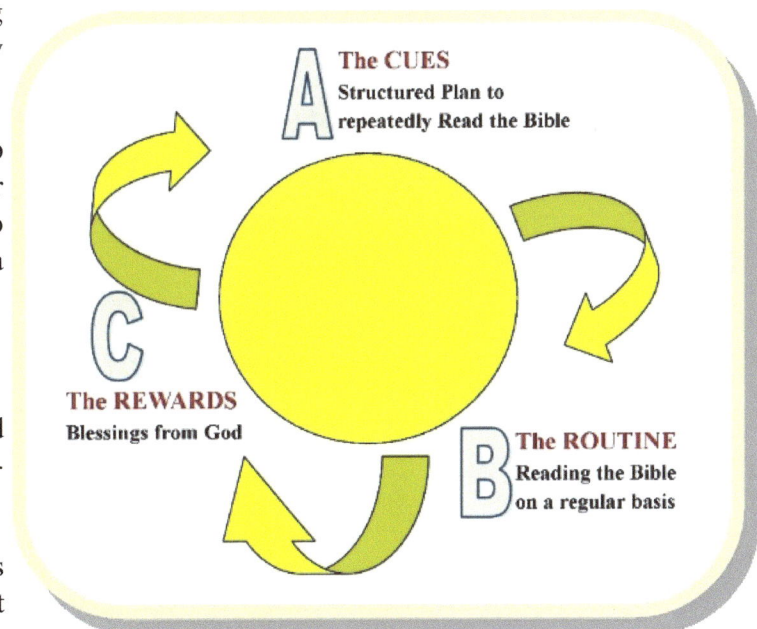

The CUES
Structured Plan to
repeatedly Read the Bible

The REWARDS
Blessings from God

The ROUTINE
Reading the Bible
on a regular basis

2nd BRM: "These Things We Believe…"

Twenty-six foundational topical statements of faith outlined the 2nd BRM. Scriptures were compiled on the basic core beliefs of New Testament Christianity. Our over-arching purpose was to let the Word of God speak for itself! Since "faith comes" from hearing (or reading) the Word of God (Romans 10:17), our contributors were told to "just let the Bible speak" on the core beliefs.

More people at Central Avenue signed up for the 2nd BRM (207) and, a church in South Carolina, one in Alabama and another in Georgia used the program. In addition, several from the Valdosta area signed up following newspaper ads.

In order to make it more interesting, those who signed up for the race were divided into two teams: the Jarvis Joggers and the Klimko Sprinters with weekly reports on the results.

3rd BRM: "Standing on the Promises of God"

"Standing on Promises of God" was the topic of the 3rd Bible Reading Marathon. Marathon runners read and studied twenty-six of the 3513 promises of God written in the Bible. These are *God's promises!* You can count of Him. "*You know with all your heart and soul that not one of all the good promises the Lord your God gave you has failed. Every promise has been fulfilled; not one has failed"* (Joshua 23:14, NIV).

Two-hundred twenty-four (224) Central members signed up to run the race. Three young men (Grady Colson, Drew Anderson, and Bryce Jackson) were team captains over the Red, Green and Blue teams. Each of these young men spoke to the congregation during the 26-week race to nudge their team members to regularly read and report their progress.

4th BRM: "Our God…An Awesome God!"

The Bible is the true story of our God. It reveals His character and divine virtues through the graphic encounters with the men and women of old. Thus, *"Our God…an Awesome God!"* was selected as the theme for the 4th Bible Reading Marathon. The modern ballad by Rich Mullins captures the emotion of the vivid images of God revealed in the Bible with such expressions as:

"There is thunder in His footsteps
And lightning in His fists
(our God is an Awesome God)."

In the opening chapters of Genesis, God is revealed as a just God. One of His fallen angels is introduced as the perennial enemy of our God. The deadly nature of sin was painted in broad strokes in the experiences of Adam and Eve when they disobeyed our God. But, the Bible also revealed the abiding hope of mercy by slowly uncovering God's divine plan of redemption. Introduced by the prophets of God, "a child was born" to bring that plan to the earth.

Three stalwart 90+ year-old-Christians (Ruth Babb, Al Little, and Louie Flythe, Sr.) were the symbolic captains for 4th BRM. Their life-size images encouraged their team members to finish the race.

Without doubt, there is a huge gap between the thinking of God and our thoughts. God thinks on a level far beyond human comprehension. Yet, He is willing to give us the tools to read His mind and begin to think like He thinks! God has not left humanity without a portal into His thinking. He inspired the books of the Bible to reveal His mind. Regular Bible reading is the process by which we mine those precious jewels from the very mind of God.

5th BRM: "Ask…for the Old Paths"

The theme for the 5th Bible Reading Marathon is *"'ask . . . for the Old Paths' - Bible Questions Answered."* All the readings for BRM 5 focused on actual questions taken directly from the Bible, such as one of the most important questions, *"Sirs, what must I do to be saved?"* (Acts 16:30). The prophet Jeremiah pleaded with his people to return to God: *"Thus said the LORD, Stand you in the ways, and see, and ask for the old paths, where is the good way, and walk therein, and you shall find rest for your souls. But they said, We will not walk therein. (Jeremiah 6:16 NKJV).*

It is easy to forget God amidst the glitter of work, fun and even religion. We are a busy people! Too busy! If we can't find time to listen to the voice of God through the words of the Bible, then *we are too busy!*

That's what the BRM is all about! It is a scheduled plan to help us get back to God if we have forgotten Him. But, it is also a daily exercise to help us maintain our connection to Him. In addition, reading the Bible will just make us better people! God's Word truly is a "lamp" that lights our paths. The Bible says:

This is the message we have heard from him and declare to you: God is light; in him there is no darkness at all. If we claim to have fellowship with him and yet walk in the darkness, we lie and do not live out the truth. But if we walk in the light, as he is in the light, we have fellowship with one another, and the blood of Jesus, his Son, purifies us from all sin (1 John 1:5-7 NKJV).

One hundred fifty-five (155) signed up to run in the 5th Bible Reading Marathon. This twenty-six-week reading plan explored some of the important questions asked in the Bible. Six young men were selected to serve as Team Captains (Kye Parker, Will Herring, Joseph Bell, Michael Herring, Jack Ricks, and Paul Farnum).

6th BRM: "Images of the Master"

The theme of the 6th BRM included everything the Apostle of John wrote in the Bible, i.e., *The Gospel of John, 1st 2nd and 3rd John* and the *Book of Revelation.* These passages outlined a detailed set of Scriptures that expanded, illustrated and commented on the *images of Jesus* from the words of John. The miracle of the ages is revealed in this simple statement: *"The Word became flesh and dwelt among us, the only begotten of the Father, full of grace and truth* (John 1:14*)."*

No one captured this image of God in the flesh more clearly than John, one of the twelve disciples. John was one of the first converts called to follow Him, and the last of his chosen twelve disciples to die.

But the prevailing image of the Master John saw was: *"God is love* (1 John 4:7-21)." The message of the Master is the story of God's love. *"This is how God showed his love among us: He sent his one and only Son into the world that we might live through him* (1 John 4:9)."

This is love: not that we loved God, but that he loved us and sent his Son as an atoning sacrifice for our sins. Dear friends, since God so loved us, we also ought to love one another. No one has ever seen God; but if we love one another, God lives in us and his love is made complete in us.

In this Bible Reading Marathon we saw *the Master* through the eyes of John, who *was an eyewitness to His majesty* while we read the Gospel of John, 1st, 2nd and 3rd John, and Revelation.

One hundred eighty-six (186) signed up for the race at Central. Two teams of young men composed of Noah Warren, Scotty Smith, Brooks Page, Mac Bowling, Alan Ferguson and Louie McMullen were team captains. Each of the captains spoke to the congregation during the weeks of the race to encourage continual reading.

7th BRM: "God's Eternal Scheme of Redemption"

The 7th BRM explains the mystery of the ages, how God revealed His plan to save man from sin and redeem us from the bondage of death. The answer is simple, …and over time, very complex! God so loved the world that he sent his one and only son to sacrifice his life in atonement for our sins. By His blood, we are redeemed from bondage and born again as children of God.

That's the short simple answer. However, the story of salvation runs from the garden of Eden in Genesis to the streets of gold in Revelation. *What* saves us from sin is simple: the love of God through the Gospel of grace. *How* we access that saving grace is the message of the entire Bible, God's inspired Word.

God's Eternal Scheme of Redemption is a compilation of scriptures beginning with creation and ending in the glories of our heavenly home. In the meantime, the Word of God is *"a lamp unto our feet"* so that we can *"walk in the light."* In these scriptures we find God's plan of salvation from sin through the Gospel of Christ.

Make the Commitment!

The Bible Reading Marathon is designed for the young Bible reader as well as the more mature experienced student of God's Word. And, it includes all of us who are in between these two! Just select the "lane" you wish to run and make the commitment to read regularly.

⇒The *INSIDE TRACK* is for those who choose to read short passages of Scripture.

⇒The *MIDDLE LANES* schedule readings that summarize the topic of the week with narratives and longer passages of Scripture. Most runners will exercise in the *MIDDLE LANES*.

⇒The *FAST TRACK* requires the most time and discipline. It is for those who are really serious about developing a regular habit of Bible reading. If you take the *FAST TRACK* you will read all the Scriptures in the *INSIDE TRACK*, the *MIDDLE LANES* and the *FAST TRACK*!

Yes! I want to join others in this spiritual exercise by entering the 7th BRM. I hereby promise that I will dedicate the time and the effort to finish the race. If I get behind, or temporarily drop out, I understand that all I have to do is just re-enter at the current reading. (I also understand that others may enter the race on any given Sunday after it has started.)

A weekly progress report may be given every Sunday morning, or, if you are out of town, call the church office and report that you are up-to-date on the readings.

I hereby make the commitment to enter the 7th BRM race: _____

(Signed/Date:_____)

Have you heard...

THE GOOD NEWS OF JESUS CHRIST!

The Gospel

Mark 16:15 ESV

And He said to them, "Go into all the world and proclaim the gospel to the whole creation."

Good News

Luke 2:8-11 ESV

And in the same region there were shepherds out in the field, keeping watch over their flock by night. And an angel of the Lord appeared to them, and the glory of the Lord shone around them, and they were filled with great fear. And the angel said to them, "Fear not, for behold, I bring you good news of great joy that will be for all the people. For unto you is born this day in the city of David a Savior, who is Christ the Lord. And this will be a sign for you: you will find a baby wrapped in swaddling cloths and lying in a manger."

God's Power to Save

Romans 1:16 ESV

For I am not ashamed of the gospel, for it is the power of God for salvation to everyone who believes, to the Jew first and also to the Greek.

Beware of False Gospels

Galatians 1:6-9 ESV

I am astonished that you are so quickly deserting him who called you in the grace of Christ and are turning to a different gospel— not that there is another one, but there are some who trouble you and want to distort the gospel of Christ. But even if we or an angel from heaven should preach to you a gospel contrary to the one we preached to you, let him be accursed. As we have said before, so now I say again: If anyone is preaching to you a gospel contrary to the one you received, let him be accursed.

You Must Obey the Gospel to be Saved

1 Peter 4:17 ESV

For it is time for judgment to begin at the household of God; and if it begins with us, what will be the outcome for those who do not obey the gospel of God? And "If the righteous is scarcely saved, what will become of the ungodly and the sinner?"

2 Thessalonians 1:7-9 ESV

And to grant relief to you who are afflicted as well as to us, when the Lord Jesus is revealed from heaven with his mighty angels in flaming fire, inflicting vengeance on those who do not know God and on those who do not obey the gospel of our Lord Jesus. They will suffer the punishment of eternal destruction, away from the presence of the Lord and from the glory of his might,

The First Gospel Sermon...

"You men of Israel, hear these words. Jesus of Nazareth, a man approved by God to you by mighty works and wonders and signs which God did by him in the midst of you, even as you yourselves know, him, being delivered up by the determined counsel and foreknowledge of God, you have taken by the hand of lawless men, crucified and killed; whom God raised up, having freed him from the agony of death, because it was not possible that he should be held by it. For David says concerning him, 'I saw the Lord always before my face, For he is on my right hand, that I should not be moved. Therefore my heart was glad, and my tongue rejoiced. Moreover my flesh also will dwell in hope; Because you will not leave my soul in Hades, Neither will you allow your Holy One to see decay. You made known to me the ways of life. You will make me full of gladness with your presence.' "Brothers, I may tell you freely of the patriarch David, that he both died and was buried, and his tomb is with us to this day. Therefore, being a prophet, and knowing that God had sworn with an oath to him that of the fruit of his body, according to the flesh, he would raise up the Christ to sit on his throne, he foreseeing this spoke about the resurrection of the Christ, that neither was his soul left in Hades, nor did his flesh see decay. This Jesus God raised up, whereof we all are witnesses. Being therefore exalted by the right hand of God, and having received from the Father the promise of the Holy Spirit, he has poured forth this, which you now see and hear. For David didn't ascend into the heavens, but he says himself, 'The Lord said to my Lord, "Sit by my right hand, Until I make your enemies the footstool of your feet."' "Let all the house of Israel therefore know assuredly that God has made him both Lord and Christ, this Jesus whom you crucified." Now when they heard this, they were cut to the heart, and said to Peter and the rest of the apostles, "Brothers, what will we do?" Peter said to them, "Repent, and be baptized, everyone of you, in the name of Jesus Christ for the forgiveness of sins, and you will receive the gift of the Holy Spirit. For to you is the promise, and to your children, and to all who are far off, even as many as the Lord our God will call to himself." With many other words he testified, and exhorted them, saying, "Save yourselves from this crooked generation!" Then those who gladly received his word were baptized. There were added that day about three thousand souls.

- Acts 2:22-41 WEB

WEEK 1
Sin and the Promised Seed of the Woman

Dates:

_____to_____

Don't let your worries get the best of you; Remember, Moses started out as a basket case.

MONDAY
LIFE IN PARADISE

Adam and Eve, first man and woman, were both created holy and happy and placed in the Garden, furnished with all the things that pertain to life and godliness. One negative command: "Don't eat of the Tree of Knowledge of Good and Evil."

TUESDAY
SATAN ENTERED

Satan, in the form of a serpent, weakened their faith in the Word of God by his cunning and devious speech. Pride prompted Satan's appeal to God's creation and pride motivated Adam and Eve to become disobedient. They sinned.

WEDNESDAY
SIN AND THE BONDAGE OF DEATH

They were cast out of the Garden and God's presence with dire consequences of life due to their sins. Ultimately, death is the penalty for sin.

THURSDAY
WAR BETWEEN GOOD AGAINST EVIL

Eternal hostility between Satan and the "seed" of the woman is predicted. Satan would inflict some painful blows, but the seed of the woman would crush Satan in the end. God promised that "good" would eventually defeat "evil."

FRIDAY
PROMISE OF REDEMPTION FROM BONDAGE

Christ, as the Seed of the woman, has paid the penalty for our sins. The Scheme of Redemption is the historical plan that pivots on the cross of Christ as promised by God. It is the story, a developed plan, of how God redeemed us from the powers of evil to serve the living God.

INSIDE TRACK	MIDDLE LANES	FAST TRACK
☐ 2 Corinthians 11:3	☐ Genesis 3:1-6	☐ Genesis 2:15-17
	☐ John 8:42-47	☐ Psalm 16:7-11
	☐ Revelation 12:7-9	☐ Matthew 1:18-25
		☐ Acts 2:23-33
		☐ 1 John 3:8-10
☐ Luke 10:18	☐ Revelation 20:1-3	☐ Job 1:6-12
	☐ 1 Timothy 2:11-15	☐ Isaiah 14:12-15
	☐ Romans 5:12-19	☐ Matthew 12:22-30
		☐ Mark 3:22-30
		☐ 1 Peter 5:8-9
☐ Romans 3:23	☐ Romans 8:18-23	☐ Numbers 16:15-40
	☐ 1 Corinthians 15:20-28	☐ Psalms 38:3 -18
	☐ Galatians 3:15-22	☐ Ezekiel 33:10 -11
		☐ Romans 4:7-8
		☐ Romans 6:15-23
☐ Romans 6:23	☐ Genesis 3:7-24	☐ Psalm 14 :1-7
	☐ Ephesians 1:3-14	☐ Isaiah 59:1-21
	☐	☐ Luke 12:22-34
		☐ 2 Corinthians 2:5-11
		☐ Philippians 1:27-30
☐ 2 Peter 3:9	☐ Revelation 12:1-17	☐ Proverbs 14:1-21
	☐ Romans 8:28-30	☐ Isaiah 53:1-12
	☐ Romans 11:33-36	☐ John 3:14-17
		☐ Romans 5:1-9
		☐ 1 Timothy 2:1-7

BE CONVERTED...

Jesus said, "Unless you are converted ...you will not enter the kingdom of heaven" (Matthew 18:3). Jesus also said, "Therefore go and make disciples of all nations, baptizing them in the name of the Father and of the Son and of the Holy Spirit, and teaching them to obey everything I have commanded you." (Matthew 28:19-20). That is the only way!

Conversion means "to turn" from sin. It is a spiritual turning which involves a new birth based on faith and repentance. It involves turning from the world values to God's values. Conversion to Christ is an about-face, in order to enter through the narrow gate that leads to eternal life.

Most of all, conversion involves change. A person has a change of mind, an intellectual change based on faith. It means a change of affection, loving God above all else. And, true conversion means a change of will, an intentional decision to turn away from sin and turn toward God through Christ. True conversion is faith in action.

Nonetheless, Jesus also said, "Not everyone ... will enter the kingdom of heaven, but only the one who does the will of my Father who is in heaven" (Matthew 7:21).

The purpose of conversion is to bring us into a right relationship with God.

* * *

"Your Stories" are actual accounts of people who have been converted to Christ. Yet, sadly, many who are unconverted will hear: 'I never knew you. Away from me, you evildoers!' (Matthew 7:23).

Growing Panes

No. 7-001

WEEK 2
Institution of the Sacrifice for Sin

DATES

_____ TO _____

Many folks want to serve God, But only as advisers.

Monday
Origin of Sacrifice

Sacrificing is of Divine origin. In the very beginning God commanded sacrifices. By faith Abel, informed by God, offered a sacrifice that was accepted. Cain also offered a sacrifice, but it was rejected. One would assume that information was given on how and what to sacrifice.

Tuesday
Sacrifices and Covenants

Sacrificing was often used to validate a covenant between God and man. Since "the life" was in the blood, a bloody sacrifice symbolized offering the most valuable things possessed. Under the Old Testament covenant, only clean animals could be offered. They foreshadowed the future.

Wednesday
Sacrifices as Shadows

Most of the sacrifices were mere *types* or *shadows* (faint outline-picture) pertaining to the future. For example, the paschal lamb or the sin-offering was a type of Christ. Like parables, the command to sacrifice illustrated the importance of faith and obedience in God's plan.

Thursday
Sin Offering

The sin offering sacrifice both atoned for the sins of the people and foreshadowed the death of Christ on the cross. The difference is that the sacrifice of Christ completely atoned the sins whereas the sin offering of the old covenant had to be offered every year.

Friday
Sacrifice of Christ

God sacrificed His one and only son on the cross. He was the perfect paschal lamb. His blood was sprinkled on the New Covenant; and salvation could be proclaimed for everyone.

INSIDE TRACK	MIDDLE LANES	FAST TRACK
☐ Genesis 4:3-5	☐ Genesis 4:1-7	☐ Genesis 8:15-22
	☐ Hebrews 11:1-4	☐ Genesis 12:1-8
	☐ Romans 10:14-18	☐ Genesis 22:1-14
		☐ Exodus 12:21-28
		☐
☐ Psalm 50:5-6	☐ Genesis 7:1-4	☐ Genesis 15:6-11
	☐ Hebrews 9:16-22	☐ Exodus 29:35-41
	☐ 1 Corinthians 10:1-13	☐ Deuteronomy 16:1-6
		☐ Galatians 3:15-29
		☐
☐ Hebrews 10:1-4	☐ Jeremiah 13:1-7	☐ Jeremiah 13:8-11
	☐ Hebrews 10:1-18	☐ Philippians 2:14-18
	☐ Ezekiel 37:1-14	☐ Hebrews 9:1-15
		☐ Hebrews 9:22-28
		☐
☐ Hebrews 9:27-28	☐ Leviticus 4:1-35	☐ Leviticus 5:7-13
	☐ Leviticus 9:1-10	☐ Romans 8:1-13
	☐	☐ Hebrews 13:11-16
		☐ Hebrews 9:6-10
		☐
☐ John 3:16-17	☐ 1 Peter 1:13-25	☐ John 3:16-21
	☐ Hebrews 5:1-10	☐ Romans 3:21-31
	☐	☐ 1 Corinthians 11:23-26
		☐ Hebrews 9:11-15
		☐ Hebrews 13:20-21

YOUR STORY..

Loneliness led Cheryle to reach out to God. Cheryle's husband was away in the Air Force and most of her childhood friends had moved away or had husbands and children of their own. Having grown up with four siblings, the quiet and solitude began to take a toll.

Cheryle had always believed in God, but during this time of aloneness, she realized she needed His presence – and His comfort. *"I began to pray for help and strength and to read the Bible. Before that time in my life, I had always thought that if you believed in God and Jesus and were a 'good' person, you would go to heaven. But as I read, I found scriptures that challenged that belief,"* she said.

In daily letters, Cheryle told her husband of things she was reading in the Bible, and when he returned home, they searched for the truth together. Cheryle's brother invited them to study with the friend who converted him, and they accepted. J.C. McMullen showed them the Jule Miller filmstrips, and answered their questions concerning salvation. Later that night, both Cheryle and her husband made the decision to be baptized.

Cheryle says the hardest year of her life turned out to be a blessing from God. Without that difficult year, she and her husband might not have been saved.

~Cheryl, 70

Growing Panes
No. 7-002

Week 3
Abraham and the Covenant of Circumcision

Don't put a question mark where God put a period.

INSIDE TRACK	MIDDLE LANES	FAST TRACK

Monday
Sacrifice and Abraham's Offspring

The promise to Abraham was that through his "seed" all nations would be blessed. Then, one of the most poignant narratives is when Abraham was commanded to sacrifice his son. This event foreshadowed God offering His son, Jesus, on the cross.

Tuesday
Circumcision and Abraham's Seeds

The covenant of circumcision was to separate Abraham and his descendants from the rest of the world and to serve as a sign/seal of the Old Covenant. Today, Christians are identified as "God's people" and the spiritual seed of Abraham.

Wednesday
Abraham's Everlasting Possession

God promised to bless Abraham. His seed according to the flesh would become a great nation. He was promised a land. Through Christ as his seed, all nations of the earth would be blessed. Today the blessings of Abraham are available through the Gospel to both Jews and Gentiles.

Thursday
All Nations Blessed through Abraham

The Gentiles were to be a part of God's Scheme of Redemption even thought the Jews resisted. The Apostle Paul was called to reach out to the Gentiles, although he was a Jew, with the message that Christ is the way of salvation for both.

Friday
God and Abraham's "Seed"

Christ is the end of the promise made to Abraham as the "seed." Today, Christians are children of Abraham by faith. Baptism corresponds to the covenant of circumcision identifying Christians as God's people.

INSIDE TRACK
- [ ] Genesis 22:15-17
- [ ] Genesis 17:10-12
- [ ] Genesis 15:4-6
- [ ] Acts 13:26-30
- [ ] Romans 4:9-12

MIDDLE LANES
- [ ] Genesis 22:1-19
- [ ] Romans 2:17-29
- [ ] Philippians 3:1-6
- [ ] Genesis 17:1-27
- [ ] Colossians 2:9-12
- [ ] Genesis 21:1-7
- [ ] Genesis 15:1-21
- [ ] Deuteronomy 1:1-48
- [ ] Numbers 34:1-18
- [ ] Acts 13:16-39
- [ ] Luke 2:1-21
- [ ] Acts 5:29-39
- [ ] Genesis 12:1-9
- [ ] Romans 4:9-25
- [ ] Galatians 3:15-22

FAST TRACK
- [ ] Genesis 17:15-22
- [ ] John 19:16-22
- [ ] Hebrews 13:11-15
- [ ] James 1:12-18
- [ ]
- [ ] Exodus 12:43-50
- [ ] Leviticus 12:1-7
- [ ] Luke 1:54-66
- [ ] Philippians 3:4-11
- [ ]
- [ ] Exodus 32:9-16
- [ ] Nehemiah 9:5-10
- [ ] Acts 7:2-8
- [ ]
- [ ]
- [ ] Exodus 6:1-8
- [ ] Deuteronomy 7:9-16
- [ ] Acts 10:34-48
- [ ] Acts 11:1-18
- [ ]
- [ ] Galatians 3:6-14
- [ ] Exodus 33:1-6
- [ ] Psalm 105:8-15
- [ ]
- [ ]

YOUR STORY...

Just to be certain, Chip was immersed twice.

"Randy wasn't sure I went all the way under the first time," he says.

Having been raised by godly parents, Chip was very familiar with church going and striving to live right. His parents instilled in him a love for God and a drive to study and learn. It was that drive to study and learn that set him on a surprise course of conversion following a visit to the Homerville congregation of his wife-to-be.

Suddenly, Chip needed to be certain about his salvation.

"I was struck by how different the church seemed, with a cappella music and weekly communion. As I studied to show how my past religious traditions were correct, I studied myself into realizing the church of Christ was where I needed to be.

I believe that if you are sincere, God will lead you to the truth." Chip believes that God used the examples of others — his wife and her parents, primarily — to give him a clearer, fuller understanding of God's plan for his life.

Chip is so very thankful for his salvation . . . and now, he is also certain.

~Chip, 53

Growing Panes

No. 7-003

Week 4
Moses and the Covenant of Law

God doesn't call the qualified, He qualifies the called.

INSIDE TRACK	MIDDLE LANES	FAST TRACK
☐ Deuteronomy 5:1-8	☐ Galatians 3:1-14	☐ Exodus 19:5-7
	☐ 1 Timothy 1:3-11	☐ Deuteronomy 6:1-6
	☐ Romans 7:7-25	☐ Acts 8:26-35
		☐ Acts 17:1-4
		☐ Luke 2:45-50
☐ Galatians 3:19-20	☐ Exodus 2:1-22	☐ Romans 10:5-10
	☐ Exodus 3:1-22	☐ Leviticus 19:1-4
	☐ Exodus 4:1-31	☐ Exodus 39:32-43
		☐ Numbers 7:1-5
		☐ Leviticus 20:22-24
☐ 1 Peter 5:8-9	☐ Exodus 5:1-9	☐ Romans 9:14-23
	☐ Exodos 6:1-12	☐ Exodus 11:9-10
	☐ Exodus 7:1-13	☐ Exodus 12:27-32
		☐ Exodus 13:17-22
		☐ Psalm 46:1-9
☐ Acts 5:11-12	☐ Exodus 7:14-8:30	☐ Mark 9:1
	☐ Exodus 9:1-33	☐ Mark 13:24-27
	☐ Exodus 10:1-29	☐ Luke 4:31-37
		☐ Luke 10:16-20
		☐ Psalm 64:1-7
☐ Romans 1:24-25	☐ Exodus 11:1-9	☐ Romans 13:10-14
	☐ Romans 6:15-23	☐ Galatians 3:13-18
	☐	☐ 2 Thessalonians 2:1-17
		☐ Romans 6:1-11
		☐ Ephesians 6:10-19

Monday
Design of the Law

The Law came about four hundred years after God promised to bless the "seed" of Abraham. The Decalogue was the constitution for Israel and revealed the moral principles required. It was designed to reveal sin to be sin. But, when that purpose ended, the law was abolished.

Tuesday
Mission of Moses

Moses was chosen by God to deliver His people from Egyptian bondage. He was to lead them through the wilderness and become the great law-giver. His mission Call illustrates our reluctance to trust God. It also illustrates how God uses people to do His Will.

Wednesday
Let My People Go

Pharaoh is indicative of the hard task-master of sin and evil, Satan. God's people requested that they be allowed to leave Egypt to go sacrifice. But, Pharaoh "hardened his heart" and refused to let them go. The forces of evil and the forces of good openly challenged!

Thursday
God's Plagues of Power

Moses and Aaron demonstrated God's power in Pharaoh's presence, but his magicians seem to have equal power. This battle played out with ten plagues inflicted on the Egyptians. The power of Satan is great, but the power of God is greater!

Friday
Slaves of Sin

God's people must do battle with the forces of evil. We are either slaves of sin or devout servants of God. Sin enslaves a person. True children of Abraham have been delivered from bondage and walk in the freedom of Christ.

YOUR STORY...

It didn't matter that he was in Seoul, Korea. After studying the Bible and determining to become a Christian, what mattered to Richard was that he get baptized as soon as possible.

Traveling six hours in a jeep along mostly dirt roads, heading to a meeting with a group of total strangers in a foreign country, completely unaware of and unconcerned about the baptismal accommodations that likely awaited him, Richard was not deterred. He simply understood that these would be necessary steps on his journey to becoming a committed Christian.

But, as a First Lieutenant in the Army stationed at a remote missile and radar site on a peninsula in the Yellow Sea, with a shortage of missile qualified officers at that site, Richard had no choice but to wait. Finally, more than a month after making his decision to be baptized, a helpful woman with the USO put Richard in contact with a small group of Christians near Seoul. One of the members retrieved Richard from the base and drove him to a Wednesday night Bible class. "They were studying from the Book of Acts, " Richard recalls, "and it fit right into my plan to be baptized."

Because this small congregation did not have a place for Richard to be baptized, they journeyed on to another building. On March 29, 1972, just shy of 27 years old, Richard committed to live the rest of his life trying to do the will of God, and was baptized in an unheated pool of water in an unfamiliar place in Seoul, Korea. Richard will tell you that the conversion matters, the details do not.

"What matters," he said, "is that nothing should stand in the way of our obedience to the gospel . . . always remember . . . life here is a means to the end, a home in Heaven." ~Richard, 73

Growing Panes
No. 7-004

Do You...

BELIEVE IN JESUS, THE CHRIST

Jesus Died for our Sins

1 Corinthians 15:1-3 ESV

Now I would remind you, brothers, of the gospel I preached to you, which you received, in which you stand, and by which you are being saved, if you hold fast to the word I preached to you—unless you believed in vain.

For I delivered to you as of first importance what I also received: that Christ died for our sins in accordance with the Scriptures,

Isaiah 53:4-6 ESV

Surely he has borne our griefs
and carried our sorrows;
yet we esteemed him stricken,
smitten by God, and afflicted.
But he was pierced for our transgressions;
he was crushed for our iniquities;
upon him was the chastisement that brought us peace,
and with his wounds we are healed.
All we like sheep have gone astray;
we have turned—every one—to his own way;
and the LORD has laid on him
the iniquity of us all.

Jesus was Buried and Raised from the Grave

1 Corinthians 15:4-8 ESV

that he was buried, that he was raised on the third day in accordance with the Scriptures, and that he appeared to Cephas, then to the twelve. Then he appeared to more than five hundred brothers at one time, most of whom are still alive, though some have fallen asleep. Then he appeared to James, then to all the apostles. Last of all, as to one untimely born, he appeared also to me.

1 Corinthians 15:14-15 ESV

And if Christ has not been raised, then our preaching is in vain and your faith is in vain. We are even found to be misrepresenting God, because we testified about God that he raised Christ, whom he did not raise if it is true that the dead are not raised.

Jesus is Lord and Savior

Ephesians 1:15-23 ESV

For this reason, because I have heard of your faith in the Lord Jesus and your love toward all the saints, ... and what is the immeasurable greatness of his power toward us who believe, according to the working of his great might that he worked in Christ when he raised him from the dead and seated him at his right hand in the heavenly places, far above all rule and authority and power and dominion, and above every name that is named, not only in this age but also in the one to come.

Acts 2:36 ESV

Let all the house of Israel therefore know for certain that God has made him both Lord and Christ, this Jesus whom you crucified

1 Peter 3:22 ESV

Jesus Christ, who has gone into heaven and is at the right hand of God, with angels, authorities, and powers having been subjected to him.

The Philippian Jailer Converted

But about midnight Paul and Silas were praying and singing hymns to God, and the prisoners were listening to them. 26 Suddenly there was a great earthquake, so that the foundations of the prison were shaken; and immediately all the doors were opened, and everyone's bonds were loosened. 27 The jailer, being roused out of sleep and seeing the prison doors open, drew his sword and was about to kill himself, supposing that the prisoners had escaped. 28 But Paul cried with a loud voice, saying, "Don't harm yourself, for we are all here!"

29 He called for lights and sprang in, and, fell down trembling before Paul and Silas, 30 and brought them out and said, "Sirs, what must I do to be saved?" 31 They said, "Believe in the Lord Jesus Christ, and you will be saved, you and your house." 32 They spoke the word of the Lord to him, and to all who were in his house. 33 He took them the same hour of the night, and washed their stripes, and was immediately baptized, he and all his household. 34 He brought them up into his house, and set food before them, and rejoiced greatly, with all his house, having believed in God.

-Acts 16:26-34 WEB

WEEK 5
The Passover and Delivery from Slavery

DATES

_____ TO _____

The task ahead of us is never as great as the Power behind us.

INSIDE TRACK	MIDDLE LANES	FAST TRACK
☐ Exodus 12:26-27	☐ Exodus 12:1-30	☐ Deuteronomy 15:19-23
	☐ Deuteronomy 16:1-8	☐ Numbers 33:1-4
	☐ Numbers 9:1-13	☐ 2 Kings 23:19-25
		☐ Deuteronomy 17:1-13
		☐ Mark 14:12-16
☐ John 1:29-30	☐ 2 Chronicles 30:1-27	☐ 2 Chronicles 35:1-6
	☐	☐ John 1:1-34
	☐	☐ Acts 8:26-40
		☐ Revelation 5:1-12
		☐ Hebrews 9:11-14
☐ Nehemiah 8:10	☐ Leviticus 23:1-44	☐ Deuteronomy 15:1-11
	☐ Numbers 28:1-31	☐ Nehemiah 8:1-18
	☐	☐ Joshua 5:1-12
		☐ Acts 20:7-11
		☐ 1 Corinthians 16:1-4
☐ Deuteronomy 16:1	☐ Exodus 19:1-25	☐ Deuteronomy 16:18-22
	☐ Deuteronomy 9:1-29	☐ Romans 6:1-23
	☐ Hebrews 8:6-13	☐ Leviticus 26:11-46
		☐ Deuteronomy 11:1-12
		☐ Joshua 22:1-6
☐ 1 Peter 1:18-19	☐ 1 Peter 1:13-25	☐ Jeremiah 31:31-34
	☐ 1 Corinthians 5:6-13	☐ 1 Corinthians 10:16-18
	☐ Matthew 27:45-54	☐ Isaiah 53:1-12
		☐ Matthew 26:17-56
		☐ 1 Peter 2:13-25

Monday
The Passover

The Passover was the first of many Old Testament commemorative institutions that served as monuments to Christ in the Scheme of Redemption. God "passed over" the children of Israel while he smote the first-born of the Egyptians. The house of Pharaoh was not spared.

Tuesday
The Paschal Lamb

A lamb without blemish was killed between "two evenings." Not a bone was to be broken. The blood from the lamb was to be sprinkled on the door posts and lintel of their houses. The blood signified deliverance of the Israelites from the death angel.

Wednesday
Appointed Festivals

Special days and festivals that the Israelites were commanded to observe foreshadowed many of the events concerning Christian behavior. They were to put these thing, first. On these days they were commanded to drop all usual activities and observe the day.

Thursday
The Law of Moses

The Law of Moses was the _Magna Carta_ for the Jews. These constitutions codified the ideal life God expected from the Jews...a standard no man except Jesus could meet! Serving as a moral and civil government, the Law sought to maintain the worship and reverence for the only true god.

Friday
Christ, Our Paschal Lamb

Sacrificing an unblemished lamb was a biblical type in the Scheme of Redemption to illustrate the sacrifice of Christ on the cross.

THE SACRIFICE...

When John saw Jesus coming, he announced, _"Behold! The Lamb of God who takes away the sin of the world"_ (John 1:29)!

God knew before the earth even existed that a sacrifice was going to be necessary, and that is why Jesus is said to _"be slain before the foundation of the earth."_ (Revelation 13:8). He was submissive even when they were nailing Him to the cross.

Jesus was _"Like a sheep...led to the slaughter and like a lamb before its shearer is silent, so he opens not his mouth"_ (Acts 8:32), and this sacrificial Lamb was foretold thousands of years before He came to the earth (Isaiah 53:7). In the Old Testament the lambs that were to be sacrificed could have no blemishes at all (Ex 12:5) and so Jesus, was sinless, without blemish, the Lamb of God.

Obedient believers are _"redeemed from the empty way of life handed down to you from your ancestors, but with the precious blood of Christ, a lamb without blemish or defect"_ (2 Peter 1:18-20).

Paul states, _"Our paschal lamb, Christ, has been sacrificed"_ (1 Corinthians 5:7). Jesus' death on the cross was a Passover from death to life for himself and for all of us. By his blood we are saved from death. Jesus made it possible for us to break out of the slavery of sin and death.

He gave us the hope of reaching our promised land, heaven.

Growing Pane

No.7-005

WEEK 6
Types and Shadows, *Then* and *Now*

DATES

_____ TO _____

God promises a safe landing, not a calm passage.

Monday
The Tabernacle

Legal biblical types provide a beautiful picture of the Christian system. The primary design of the tabernacle was to furnish a house for God. The tabernacle is a type for Christ's church which is the temple of God. The tabernacle and the church symbolize the dwelling place for God.

Tuesday
Ark of the Covenant & Mercy Seat

The Most Holy Place was illuminated by the *Shekinah,* the glory of the Lord. This glow was over the Mercy Seat, the top of the Ark of the Covenant which housed the Tablets of Stone, a pot of Manna, and Aaron's rod that budded. God's authority is symbolized here...with mercy!

Wednesday
Altar of Incense & Candelabrum

The Altar of Incense, Golden Candelabrum, and the Table of Shew-bread were in the Holy Place. The incense was typical of the prayers of the saints. The Candelabrum symbolized the church of Christ as God's appointed means of sending the light of the Gospel to a lost world.

Thursday
Table of Shewbread

The Shew-bread suggests Christ as the bread of life. Symbolically, Christians *eat* of the body of Christ when we partake of the Lord's Supper. It was eaten only by the priests; symbolizes the spiritual food of Christians who also are priests of God.

Friday
Burnt-Offering Altar/Brazen Laver

The Brazen Laver was for *cleansing,* symbolic of baptism and the moral and spiritual purity of a baptized believer. God's appointed place for sacrifices was on the Burnt-Offering altar. Sacrificing was very important in the Scheme of Redemption.

INSIDE TRACK	MIDDLE LANES	FAST TRACK
John 1:14	Exodus 26:1-37	Hebrews 8:3-13
	Exodus 36:1-38	Hebrews 9:11-15
	1 Corinthians 3:10-17	Acts 7:44-50
		Revelation 15:5-8
		Revelation 21:1-4
Hebrews 1:1-2	Exodus 25:10-16	Exodus 25:17-22
	Exodus 37:1-9	Hebrews 1:1-4
	Romans 9:1-5	Romans 3:23-26
		John 14:9
Psalm 141:1-2	Exodus 30:1-10; 34-38	Hebrews 7:23-27
	Leviticus 24:1-4	Romans 8:31-39
	Revelation 8:1-5	Ephesians 5:1-2
		Isaiah 56:3-8
Luke 22:29-30	Exodus 25:23-30	John 6:30-40
	Leviticus 24:5-9	John 6:47-51
	1 Peter 2:4-9	1 Corinthians 10:14-17
		Luke 22:24-30
Hebrews 7:26-28	Exodus 30:17-21	Hebrews 13:11-16
	Leviticus 1:1-17	Hebrews 10:5-18
	Psalm 24:3-4	Hebrews 7:11-25

YOUR STORY...

Fear of eternal torment persuaded Rachel to be baptized 64 years ago at the age of 17.

The preacher's "fiery sermons" during a two-week spring gospel meeting scared Rachel. A huge plastic screen, blazes of fire painted on it, depicted hell, and the impassioned preacher said "people who did not obey the gospel would go there." She knew she did not want to go there. One fear was quickly replaced by another.

"I was fearful about going home and telling my parents that I was baptized at the church of Christ," she said. Her mother, father, and siblings attended other churches, and Rachel was afraid of their reaction.

But Rachel recalls being encouraged by the support she received from the neighborhood friend who had invited her to church, and later, from her Aunt Judy, a faithful Christian, who loved Rachel and treated her like her own child. *"[The church] showed so much love and interest in me,"* and that love and interest was so beneficial in her Christian walk.

Fear urged Rachel to take that first step of obedience, but fear has long since matured into a loving desire to faithfully serve the Lord, and to one day live with Him in heaven.

"The Bible is our guidebook for the Christian life," she said, and *"life is just our journey"* on the way to eternity. ~Rachel, 81

Growing Panes
No. 7-006

WEEK 7
Sacred Examples of Holiness

The best mathematical equation I have ever seen: 1 cross + 3 nails = 4 given.

DATES

_____ TO _____

Monday
Most Holy of Holies

God has always required that His people be holy. The reason is, God is Holy. Only the priests could enter the Most Holy Place; once each year when they made Atonement for the people. This inner chamber was where God met His people through the priests. It also symbolized heaven.

Tuesday
The Priesthood

The Levitical priests offered sacrifices, burned incense and performed all the other duties of the tabernacle. It was their duties to instruct the people and to act as God's ministers in all matters of mercy and benevolence. Their qualifications to serve were defined in terms of purity and holiness.

Wednesday
The Sabbath

The seventh day each week was sacred for the Jews. After the creation of the world, God rested on the seventh day. The Sabbath was made for man. There is a rest (sabbath) that remains for children of God, but there is a partial rest from the burden of sin.

Thursday
Day of Atonement

The High Priest performed, or superintended, sacrifices and other rituals on this day for all the sins of the past year. He entered the Most Holy Place after the great sin-offering for the people. In many respects this day was the most sacred of all the Sabbaths.

Friday
Other Holy Days

Many other days were set aside as holy days. One was the Feast of Weeks that continued for seven weeks and a day after Passover. It ended on the first day of the week, or Pentecost.

INSIDE TRACK
- [ ] Hebrews 9:24-25
- [ ] Numbers 3:3-4
- [ ] Exodus 31:12-13
- [ ] Exodus 30:10
- [ ] Exodus 23:14-16

MIDDLE LANES
- [ ] Hebrews 9:3-14
- [ ] Hebrews 10:19-39
- [ ]
- [ ] Exodus 28:1-43
- [ ] Numbers 16:1-50
- [ ] Numbers 17:1-13
- [ ] Genesis 2:1-3
- [ ] Deuteronomy 5:12-15
- [ ] Colossians 2:16-23
- [ ] Leviticus 16:1-34
- [ ] Numbers 29:7-11
- [ ] Hebrews 10:1-18
- [ ] Leviticus 23:1-44
- [ ] Deuteronomy 16:1-17
- [ ] Acts 2:1-13

FAST TRACK
- [ ] Leviticus 11:43-45
- [ ] 1 Kings 6:14-16
- [ ] Ezekiel 41:1-4
- [ ] Numbers 18:8-10
- [ ] 2 Chronicles 3:8-13
- [ ] Numbers 3:5-10
- [ ] Numbers 4:4-15
- [ ] Numbers 18:1-7
- [ ] Numbers 4:21-33
- [ ]
- [ ] Exodus 31:12-17
- [ ] Exodus 20:8-11
- [ ] Exodus 16:22-30
- [ ] Leviticus 25:1-8
- [ ] Numbers 28:9-10
- [ ] Leviticus 4:1-12
- [ ] Leviticus 5:4-10
- [ ] Leviticus 6:24-30
- [ ] Hebrews 2:10-18
- [ ] Hebrews 5:1-11
- [ ] Esther 9:20-28
- [ ] Exodus 12:1-14
- [ ] Numbers 9:1-5
- [ ] Numbers 28:16-25
- [ ] Numbers 29:1-6

YOUR STORY...

On the night Joe Gray and his family were leaving Valdosta, Georgia, to begin their missionary work in New Zealand, Janet was baptized. She was 13 years old. *"It was, without a doubt, the best decision I've ever made in my life."*

But Janet's conversion, like many conversions, really began decades earlier with a great-grandmother dedicated to serving God and determined to share the gospel.

When Janet's grandfather married her grandmother, her great-grandmother said, "I was not able to convert my son, but I will do my best to convert his wife." And she did. Janet's grandmother raised her father in the church, but when he was older, he did exactly as his father had done — he left the church.

"The spring of my fourth grade year, I was taking piano lessons, and my mother, who never believed in wasting a minute of time, would often put down the back seat of our station wagon, get back there, and cut out dresses," Janet recalled. That is where Janet's mother was when Central's minister, Bill Long, saw her and invited her to a spring gospel meeting. Janet's mother took the invitation home to her father, and thereafter, they all began attending church together.

Both of her parents were later baptized, and at the age of 80, so was her grandfather. Years ago, Janet's great-grandmother prepared the soil and planted the seeds. In time, the harvest came.

~Janet, 62

Growing Panes
No. 7-007

WEEK 8
Deliverance from Joshua to Jesus

Don't give God instructions, just report for duty!

DATES _____ TO _____

Monday
The Wilderness of Sin

The people remained at Sinai about one year. The signal then was given, the cloud was taken up from the tabernacle, and the people moved forward. God provided both water and food. All the men of fighting age would die in the Wilderness except Caleb and Joshua.

Tuesday
Idolatry

God's people were warned about idolatry which was introduced through sexual immorality. They were forbidden to neither covenant with the idol worshippers, nor to allow intermarriage. Freedom from bondage under Moses was symbolic of our deliverance from sin by Christ.

Wednesday
God's Faithfulness

God promised to go with them, but He gave them some very hard challenges. The Israelites did not always do what God said, but he was faithful. Taking the land of Canaan was a type of the final destruction of evil by fire in the last days.

Thursday
The Promised Land

Joshua, a type of Jesus, was to lead them into battle. The promised land was not free; they had to go over and "possess" it. However, the rewards were great for those whose trust was in the true God. It was truly a land that "flowed with milk and honey." Canaan was a type of heaven.

Friday
Prophecies of Jesus

The prophets spoke of the coming Messiah more than nine-hundred years prior to his birth. Jesus was to be the sacrificial lamb, the great deliverer, the King of Kings!

INSIDE TRACK
- [ ] Exodus 15:25-27
- [ ] Exodus 32:2-4
- [ ] Joshua 3:14-17
- [ ] Joshua 1:6
- [ ] Luke 1:68-75

MIDDLE LANES
- [ ] Numbers 10:1-36
- [ ] Numbers 20:1-21
- [ ] Deuteronomy 34:1-12
- [ ] Exodus 34:8-17
- [ ] Numbers 25:1-18
- [ ] 1 Corinthians 10:1-22
- [ ] Joshua 1:1-18
- [ ] Deuteronomy 20:1-20
- [ ]
- [ ] Deuteronomy 31:1-30
- [ ] Joshua 22:1-5
- [ ] Deuteronomy 19:1-10
- [ ] Hebrews 4:1-11
- [ ] Hebrews 11:8-16
- [ ] John 12:12-18

FAST TRACK
- [ ] Exodus 16:9-16
- [ ] Exodus 18:20-27
- [ ] Exodus 19:7-14
- [ ] Exodus 33:10-16
- [ ] Numbers 11:4-12
- [ ] Leviticus 26:1-6
- [ ] Exodus 20:1-5
- [ ] 1 Samuel 15:23
- [ ] Galatians 5:20
- [ ] Deuteronomy 29:16-20
- [ ] Deuteronomy 7:9-11
- [ ] Psalm 36:5-10
- [ ] Psalm 40:1-5
- [ ] Hosea 2:20-23
- [ ] Hebrews 3:5-6
- [ ] Joshua 3:1-8
- [ ] Titus 2:9-10
- [ ] Proverbs 11:13
- [ ]
- [ ]
- [ ] Matthew 12:18-21
- [ ] Mark 6:1-6
- [ ] Luke 7:24-28
- [ ] Acts 2:14-21
- [ ] John 1:20-23

YOUR STORY...

Obedience.
Simple really. The Bible commands it; she did it.

"It is the right thing - to do as we are commanded to do," Gail said. So at the age of 20, after Bible studies with her husband and with the minister, Gail knew what was required of her.

"After I had studied, I knew [baptism} was what I had to do. Joe Gray baptized me on July 19, 1968, at Central Church of Christ. My life is better. I know I have the Lord to guide me," Gail said.

Gail guided her children, rearing them in a God-fearing, Bible-believing home, teaching them that loving the Lord meant obeying the Lord. "Raising my children in a Christian home and teaching them Christian values" was Gail's most important responsibility as a parent, and having Christian children is her greatest blessing, she said.

"We are commanded to be baptized and live a Christian life and to tell others about the Lord," Gail said.

Simple really, but so significant. Obedience.
~Gail, 69

Growing Panes
No. 7-008

Commands to be Obeyed...

CONFESS YOUR FAITH IN CHRIST

Salvation is by the Grace and Mercy of God

Ephesians 2:8-9 (ESV)

For by grace you have been saved through faith. And this is not your own doing; it is the gift of God, not a result of works, so that no one may boast.

Titus 3:4-7 (ESV)

But when the goodness and loving kindness of God our Savior appeared, he saved us, not because of works done by us in righteousness, but according to his own mercy, by the washing of regeneration and renewal of the Holy Spirit, whom he poured out on us richly through Jesus Christ our Savior, so that being justified by his grace we might become heirs according to the hope of eternal life.

Confessing Faith in Christ

Romans10:8-10 (ESV)

But what does it say? "The word is near you, in your mouth and in your heart" (that is, the word of faith that we proclaim); because, if you confess with your mouth that Jesus is Lord and believe in your heart that God raised him from the dead, you will be saved. For with the heart one believes and is justified, and with the mouth one confesses and is saved.

Matthew 10:32-33 (KJV)

So everyone who acknowledges me before men, I also will acknowledge before my Father who is in heaven, but whoever denies me before men, I also will deny before my Father who is in heaven.

Called the Good Confession

Acts 8:36-37 (KJV)

And as they went on *their* way, they came unto a certain water: and the eunuch said, See, *here is* water; what doth hinder me to be baptized? And Philip said, If thou believest with all thine heart, thou mayest. And he answered and said, I believe that Jesus Christ is the Son of God.

1 Timothy 6:11-12 (KJV)

But thou, O man of God, flee these things; and follow after righteousness, godliness, faith, love, patience, meekness. Fight the good fight of faith, lay hold on eternal life, whereunto thou art also called, and hast professed a good profession before many witnesses.

Conversion of the Ethiopian Eunuch

But an angel of the Lord spoke to Philip, saying, "Arise, and go toward the south to the way that goes down from Jerusalem to Gaza. This is a desert." He arose and went; and behold, there was a man of Ethiopia, a eunuch of great authority under Candace, queen of the Ethiopians, who was over all her treasure, who had come to Jerusalem to worship. He was returning and sitting in his chariot, and was reading the prophet Isaiah. The Spirit said to Philip, "Go near, and join yourself to this chariot." Philip ran to him, and heard him reading Isaiah the prophet, and said, "Do you understand what you are reading?" He said, "How can I, unless someone explains it to me?" He begged Philip to come up and sit with him.

Now the passage of the Scripture which he was reading was this, "He was led as a sheep to the slaughter. As a lamb before his shearer is silent, so he doesn't open his mouth.

In his humiliation, his judgment was taken away. Who will declare His generation? For his life is taken from the earth."

The eunuch answered Philip, "Who is the prophet talking about? About himself, or about someone else?" Philip opened his mouth, and beginning from this Scripture, preached to him Jesus. As they went on the way, they came to some water, and the eunuch said, "Behold, here is water. What is keeping me from being baptized?" He commanded the chariot to stand still, and they both went down into the water, both Philip and the eunuch, and he baptized him.

- Acts 8:26-38 WEB

WEEK 9
Our Redeemer Introduced

Practice makes perfect, so be careful what you practice.

DATES
_____ TO _____

Monday
The Prophets Spoke

Let the last days of God's Eternal Scheme of Redemption begin when righteousness by faith will be exalted and the victory will be won. The prophets said He would come in glory to begin His final battle with sin and death. Christ came about four hundred years after the close of the O.T.

Tuesday
Parentage and Early Life

Our Redeemer was conceived by the virgin Mary in Bethlehem and grew up in Nazareth. He was a *man*, a real person having a human body and endowed with the faculties, powers, susceptibilities of human nature in its sinless state. But, he was *God* in the flesh, the *Messiah!*

Wednesday
Ministry of John

The whole scope of John's ministry was simply "to prepare a people for the coming Messiah." God's people and their leaders had forsaken the way of truth and become sinful. John neither changed any laws nor established any new institutions.

Thursday
John's Message

John's message was also simple, "Repent." After baptism the only change in their condition was a death to sin and a resurrection to a life of holiness in preparation to the coming of their anxiously awaited Messiah. His ministry ended when Herod Antipas had him beheaded.

Friday
John and Jesus

Jesus was John's cousin. John introduced and baptized Jesus, although he had no sins. John was to decrease and Jesus was to increase. Many of John's disciples became disciples of Jesus.

INSIDE TRACK	MIDDLE LANES	FAST TRACK
☐ 2 Corinthians 4:1-6	☐ Isaiah 40:1-5	☐ Isaiah 7:1-17
	☐ Malachi 3:1-5	☐ Micah 5:2-4
	☐ Malachi 4:1-6	☐ 2 Samuel 7:1-17
	☐ Isaiah 2:2-4	☐ Psalm 110:1-7
		☐ Isaiah 53:1-12
☐ Luke 2:49-50	☐ Luke 1:5-25	☐ Luke 1: 26-38
	☐ Mark 1:1-11	☐ Luke 1: 57-80
	☐ John 1:1-18	☐ Romans 3:1-8
		☐ Matthew 1:18-25
		☐ Matthew 2:1-12
☐ Matthew 11:11	☐ John 1:19-28	☐ Matthew 12:38-45
	☐ John 3:22-36	☐ Matthew 4:12-17
	☐ Luke 3:1-20	☐ Colossians 1:1-14
		☐ Matthew 14:1-12
		☐ 1 Timothy 1:1-20
☐ Acts 2:38-39	☐ Matthew 3:1-12	☐ Matthew 11:1-19
	☐ Matthew 21:23-27	☐ Acts 1:1-5
	☐	☐ Acts 19:1-7
		☐ Matthew 17:1-13
		☐ Luke 7:18-35
☐ Luke 9:18-20	☐ John 1:29-34	☐ John 18:28-40
	☐ Luke 3:21-38	☐ John 1:35-42
	☐ Matthew 3:13-17	☐ Matthew 16:13-20
		☐ Mark 8:27-30
		☐ John 11:1-44

THE MESSAGE...

The G-O-S-P-E-L message!

The question "What is the Gospel?" is the most important question a person can ask. The word *Gospel* literally means "good news."

The Gospel reveals the plan that God has designed to save sinful humans from eternal separation from Him. The Gospel story is the final page in God's eternal scheme of redemption.

The "bad news" is that "all have sinned and fall short of the glory of God (Romans 3:23)." Sin means to "miss the mark" God has set for us. The penalty for sin is death (Romans 6:23).

The Message is clear: God demonstrated His love for us by sending his "one and only" son to die for us. He came, lived a sinless life and died.

This sacrifice from Heaven paid a debt we could not pay by taking our place on the deadly hill of Calvary, nailed to a cross. The living blood of our dying savior faithfully and obediently sealed the covenant of salvation from sin.

But, three days after His death is the rest of the story: *"By this gospel you are saved, ... For what I received I passed on to you as of first importance:* [1] *that Christ died for our sins according to the Scriptures,* [2] *that he was buried,* [3] *that he was raised on the third day according to the Scriptures (1 Corinthians 15:1-3)."*

Growing Panes

No. 7-009

WEEK 10
Christ's Nature, Character and Personality

DATES

_____ TO _____

Jesus paid a debt He didn't owe because we owed a debt we couldn't pay.

Monday
Who is Christ?

We know He was God as well and man. Before He took on human flesh, He was with God, and was God. His throne is eternal. His name is the only name that brings salvation. But, as God, His ways are greater than our ways, and His thoughts are greater than our thoughts.

Tuesday
The Creative Powers of Deity

God alone has the power to create; and the Scriptures ascribe this power to Jesus. Nothing was created except by Him. Most important, he created man and the world we live in. We are His offspring, created in His image with an eternal soul.

Wednesday
The Object of Worship

In the same way we would honor and reverence Father-God, we honor Son-God. Every knee should bow to Him, both in heaven and on earth. Even the angels worship Him. Our worship, including our prayers, must ascent to the highly exalted Son.

Thursday
He Forgives Sins

Jesus forgives sins. During his ministry on earth this was one of the things he taught and did that angered the Jewish leaders. They understood that only God could forgive sins. Jesus became the sacrifice on the cross that takes away the sins of the world. His forgiveness is available to all.

Friday
One Almighty God

Our God is one god. God acts in unison as the Father, Son and the Holy Spirt. He is almighty and all-knowing; the King of Kings and the Lord of Lords. He is our Redeemer from bondage.

INSIDE TRACK	MIDDLE LANES	FAST TRACK
☐ Romans 8:38-39	☐ Isaiah 9:2-7	☐ 1 Corinthians 4:1-5
	☐ Hebrews 1:1-14	☐ Matthew 19:25-30
	☐ Matthew 16:13-20	☐ Romans 7:21-25
		☐ Romans 10:5:13
		☐ Philippians 3:4-14
☐ Genesis 1:25-27	☐ Ephesians 3:7-19	☐ Isaiah 4:17-20
	☐ Colossians 1:15-20	☐ Jeremiah 51:5-15
	☐ Revelation 21:1-27	☐ John 1:1-3
		☐ Colossians 1:4-9
		☐ Revelation 4:8-11
☐ Revelation 5:11-14	☐ John 5:16-23	☐ Matthew 4:1-11
	☐ Philippians 2:1-11	☐ Psalm 2:7-12
	☐ John 4:1-26	☐ 2 Samuel 7:5-8
		☐ Romans 1:1-7
		☐
☐ Hebrews 9:15	☐ Luke 5:17-26	☐ Colossians 3:12-17
	☐ Luke 23:32-49	☐ Matthew 6:14-15
	☐ Matthew 18:23-35	☐ Luke 17:3-4
		☐ 1 John 1:8-10
		☐ Acts 3:17-20
☐ 1 Samuel 2:1-3	☐ John 10:22-39	☐ Matthew 19:17-19
	☐ John 14:1-14	☐ Psalm 139:1-10
	☐ Job 11:7-9	☐ Psalm 90:12-17
		☐ Isaiah 47:4
		☐ 2 Samuel 7:22-29

YOUR STORY...

Knowing Jesus died on the cross for him, Jerry very much wanted to belong to His church.

So, at 13 years of age, after studying with and being influenced by great teachers in the Church, including his parents, Jerry put Christ on in baptism. *"I felt I was fully ready,"* he said. *"It was time because I knew what I needed to do."*

His Christian walk was good at first, Jerry said, but he later went through a period in his life when he was not a good example for others. Again, Jerry knew what he needed to

do. Jerry knew he had to set a Christian example. He knew that every day he needed to live his best life for Christ.

Jerry also knew, he said, that living his best life for Christ, meant *"staying in the Word"* so that he could be a good example to others and be able to *"say the right thing at the right time."*

Staying in the Word – in Christ – brings restoration and revival, Jerry said, and a clear reminder of this truth: *"God is our father and creator of all things. The only way to Heaven is through his son, Jesus Christ."*

~Jerry, 69

Growing Panes

No. 7-010

WEEK 11
Why the WORD Became Flesh
We don't change the message, the message changes us.

DATES

_____ TO _____

Monday
Seed, Satan, Sacrifice

Man sinned and it was known in Heaven, Earth, and Hell. In the fullness of time the great antitype of all the sacrifices that were ever slain appeared on the cross. The "seed" of the woman made atonement for the sins of the world. Three days later, Jesus defeated the power of Satan.

Tuesday
To Satisfy God's Justice

First, it had never been God's purpose in the Scheme of Redemption to pass over sin or the transgression of His law without a just and adequate satisfaction. Thus, the first objective of the incarnation and death of Christ was to meet and satisfy the claims of justice against the sinner.

Wednesday
To Change Sinners to Saints

Second, it was to magnify God's law and make it honorable by opening up a new and living way through which God's mercy and grace might freely and justly flow to guilty man. Thus, changing the heart of the sinner, and his rebellion, by the love of God.

Thursday
By Christ being Our Example to Follow

Third, the Word became flesh and dwelt among us to show us by his own example how we should all walk and please God. Christ made the will of His father his supreme rule of conduct. Christ was our example in his manner of meeting and overcoming temptations.

Friday
To Destroy the Works of Satan

Fourth, Christ came to destroy the works of Satan. Through the diabolical cunning temptations of the Evil One, all the earth has been taken into cruel bondage. That battle to destroy was begun on the Day of Pentecost, A.D. 33, and continues today.

INSIDE TRACK
- [ ] Acts 13:38-41
- [ ] Psalm 78:35
- [ ] Proverbs 23:17-18
- [ ] Hebrews 2:14-18
- [ ] John 16:33

MIDDLE LANES
- [ ] Hebrews 10:1-25
- [ ] Luke 24:36-49
- [ ] Revelation 12:1-17
- [ ] Romans 3:21-31
- [ ] 1 Peter 1:13-25
- [ ] 1 John 4:7-12
- [ ] 2 Corinthians 5:11-21
- [ ] Matthew 12:22-45
- [ ]
- [ ] Ephesians 5:1-20
- [ ] Hebrews 12:1-12
- [ ] 1 Thessalonians 1:4-10
- [ ] Romans 6:1-23
- [ ] 1 John 3:1-10
- [ ] Revelation 20:11-15

FAST TRACK
- [ ] Genesis 3:1-24
- [ ] Acts 5:17-42
- [ ] Ephesians 2:1-10
- [ ] 2 Timothy 1:6-18
- [ ] Mark 15:14-33
- [ ] Romans 8:18-30
- [ ] 1 Corinthians 1:26-31
- [ ] Titus 2:1-14
- [ ] 1 Peter 2:1-25
- [ ] Psalm 19:1-14
- [ ] Ephesians 1:1-14
- [ ] Galatians 3:1-29
- [ ] Hebrews 3:7-19
- [ ] James 4:1-17
- [ ] Psalm 51:1-19
- [ ] Matthew 4:1-11
- [ ] Matthew 26:36-41
- [ ] 2 Timothy 2:1-10
- [ ] James 1:1-18
- [ ] 2 Corinthians 10:11-18
- [ ] Acts 2:1-47
- [ ] 2 Thessalonians 2:1-17
- [ ] 1 John 4:1-6
- [ ] 1 John 5:1-12
- [ ] Colossians 1:1-23

YOUR STORY...

Seventeen years old and a senior in high school, Hailee had heard the gospel message many times before. This time, the message hit the mark.

When the invitation was given, Hailee boldly stepped into the aisle, and made her way to the front of the auditorium, surprising herself and her family. *"Nobody knew I was going to be baptized that day. I didn't know it myself,"* she recalls. *"I really don't know why it happened on that particular day. I just realized that no matter what, God would always love me, and I just had this strong feeling come over me and I knew I needed to go forward."*

Immediately after coming up out of the water, Hailee felt relief, she said, *"like a huge weight had been lifted off my shoulders."* Her burdens were lifted, and the future, suddenly brighter, possessed such promise. Her attitude about everything changed, she said. She is more optimistic, more confident, more encouraging.

Hailee wants everyone to know how God's love changed her life and her attitude about life. More importantly, God's love changed her future. *"It is an awesome feeling knowing that I'm going to Heaven."* Hailee really wants the world to know that.

~Hailee, 17

Growing Panes

No. 7-011

WEEK 12
The Holy Spirit in Redemption

Coincidence is when God chooses to remain anonymous.

DATES

_____ TO _____

Monday
In Conversion of Sinners

The Holy Spirit operates on the minds of the unconverted through the Word of God, and it never converts any person without the Word. It may operate on their minds in a providential way, but never without the Word of God. Hearts may be softened by the Holy Spirit.

Tuesday
Working through the Word

The gospel message of the death, burial and resurrection of Jesus is a product of the Holy Spirit. The Holy Spirit is not the Word, but the voice of the Holy Spirit. The Holy Spirit operates on the minds and hearts of men as a farmer would sow seed for harvest. The Word is the seed.

Wednesday
In Sanctifying the Saints

The Holy Spirit dwells in Christians to encourage us through the sanctification process. Commands to obey are revealed through the Word. Our love for God allows the Holy Spirit to operate. Whoever has the commands and keeps them loves God and continues to grow in the Spirit.

Thursday
Strengthens the Inner Man

The Holy Spirit operates directly, or providentially, so as to strengthen our weaknesses and to cause the Word of God to become more productive in fruits of holiness. The Holy Spirit assists us when we do not know how to pray; but in accordance with the Word of God.

Friday
Disciplines and Corrects

Even in our momentary suffering, the Spirit of faith rests on us. The power of the Holy Spirit renews our inner spirit daily. Trials and tribulations are opportunities to become stronger.

INSIDE TRACK	MIDDLE LANES	FAST TRACK
☐ Ephesians 6:17	☐ Joel 2:28-32	☐ John 15:18-27
	☐ John 16:1-11	☐ Acts 2:1-4,14-36
	☐ Titus 3:1-7	☐ 2 Corinthians 4:1-18
		☐ 1 Peter 1:10-12
		☐
☐ John 6:63	☐ John 3:1-21	☐ Nehemiah 9:1-8
	☐ Luke 8:4-15	☐ Nehemiah 9:16-31
	☐ 1 Peter 1:17-25	☐ Luke 4:14-21
		☐ 1 Corinthians 6:6-16
		☐ 2 Peter 1:16-21
☐ 2 Thess. 2:13-15	☐ Romans 8:1-17	☐ Isaiah 44:1-5
	☐ Ezekiel 36:25-27	☐ Matthew 3:1-12
	☐ John 14:15-31	☐ Romans 5:1-5
		☐ Romans 15:14-21
		☐ Galatians 5:16-26
☐ Zechariah 4:6	☐ Ephesians 1:3-23	☐ Psalm 143:3-10
	☐ Hebrews 12:4-13	☐ Haggai 2:1-9
	☐ Romans 8:18-39	☐ Ephesians 3:14-21
		☐ Colossians 1:9-14
		☐ Psalm 84:1-12
	☐ 2 Samuel 12:13-23	☐ Isaiah 42:1-9
☐ Job 5:17	☐ 1 Peter 4:12-19	☐ Isaiah 59:9-21
	☐	☐ Micah 3:5-12
		☐ Titus 3:8-11
		☐ Deuteronomy 8:1-5

YOUR STORY...

Ordinary behaviors can have extraordinary power.

Just ask Joyce, who as a young child, was introduced to Christ via bedtime stories from scripture read to her by a loving aunt. A routine act with intentional purpose helped to construct the foundation that Joyce would build her life upon. *"At a very early age my aunt read scripture to me at bedtime. This helped me to begin to know who Christ was,"* Joyce said.

Shortly after moving to Valdosta in the early 1960s, Joyce and her husband became friends with the Grants and the Paines. These two families, Joyce said, were also very influential in her quest to know Christ and live for Him. They invited Joyce and her husband to watch the Jule Miller filmstrips. After seeing the films, they decided together that they wanted to be baptized.

"We understood that we needed to be baptized to have our sins washed away and to receive the Holy Spirit," she said. So late one Sunday night, Joyce and her husband were baptized, and their *"hearts were filled with the Spirit. I have learned what it takes to be a Christian through studying the Bible and trying daily to live a Christ-like life,"* she said.

Joyce is grateful for the Christian influence of her mother, her aunt, and her friends. Their intentional acts of faith demonstrated that "living a Christ-like life" was the best way to live life.

"You have no freedom without Christ in your life. Without Christ," Joyce said, *"you have no happiness."*

~Joyce, 78

Growing Panes

No. 7-012

Commands to be Obeyed...

REPENT OF SINS

(MAKING THE DECISION TO TURN FROM OUR SINS)

Proclaim Repentance from Sin

Luke 24:45-47 (ESV)

Then he opened their minds to understand the Scriptures, and said to them, "Thus it is written, that the Christ should suffer and on the third day rise from the dead, and that repentance for the forgiveness of sins should be proclaimed in his name to all nations, beginning from Jerusalem.

A Call for Repentance

Acts 2:37-40 (ESV)

Now when they heard this they were cut to the heart, and said to Peter and the rest of the apostles, "Brothers, what shall we do?" And Peter said to them, "Repent and be baptized every one of you in the name of Jesus Christ for the forgiveness of your sins, and you will receive the gift of the Holy Spirit. For the promise is for you and for your children and for all who are far off, everyone whom the Lord our God calls to himself." And with many other words he bore witness and continued to exhort them, saying, "Save yourselves from this crooked generation."

Acts 3:17-20 (ESV)

"And now, brothers, I know that you acted in ignorance, as did also your rulers. But what God foretold by the mouth of all the prophets, that his Christ would suffer, he thus fulfilled. Repent therefore, and turn back, that your sins may be blotted out, that times of refreshing may come from the presence of the Lord,

Repent or Perish

Acts 17:26-31 (ESV)

Being then God's offspring, we ought not to think that the divine being is like gold or silver or stone, an image formed by the art and imagination of man. The times of ignorance God overlooked, but now he commands all people everywhere to repent, because he has fixed a day on which he will judge the world in righteousness by a man whom he has appointed; and of this he has given assurance to all by raising him from the dead."

Encourage Repentance

2 Timothy 2:24-25 (ESV)

As the Lord's servant, you must not quarrel. You must be kind toward all, a good and patient teacher, who is gentle as you correct your opponents, for it may be that God will give them the opportunity to repent and come to know the truth.

Saul's Obedience to the Gospel

"I am a Jew, born in Tarsus in Cilicia, but brought up in this city, educated at the feet of Gamaliel[b] according to the strict manner of the law of our fathers, being zealous for God as all of you are this day. I persecuted this Way to the death, binding and delivering to prison both men and women, as the high priest and the whole council of elders can bear me witness. From them I received letters to the brothers, and I journeyed toward Damascus to take those also who were there and bring them in bonds to Jerusalem to be punished.

I myself was convinced that I ought to do many things in opposing the name of Jesus of Nazareth. And I did so in Jerusalem. I not only locked up many of the saints in prison after receiving authority from the chief priests, but when they were put to death I cast my vote against them. And I punished them often in all the synagogues and tried to make them blaspheme, and in raging fury against them I persecuted them even to foreign cities. (Acts 26:9-11 WEB)

It happened that, as I made my journey, and came close to Damascus, about noon, suddenly there shone from the sky a great light around me. I fell to the ground, and heard a voice saying to me, 'Saul, Saul, why are you persecuting me?' I answered, 'Who are you, Lord?' He said to me, 'I am Jesus of Nazareth, whom you persecute.' "Those who were with me indeed saw the light and were afraid, but they didn't understand the voice of him who spoke to me. I said, 'What shall I do, Lord?' The Lord said to me, 'Arise, and go into Damascus. There you will be told about all things which are appointed for you to do.' When I couldn't see for the glory of that light, being led by the hand of those who were with me, I came into Damascus.

One Ananias, a devout man according to the law, well reported of by all the Jews who lived in Damascus, came to me, and standing by me said to me, 'Brother Saul, receive your sight!' In that very hour I looked up at him. He said, 'The God of our fathers has appointed you to know his will, and to see the Righteous One, and to hear a voice from his mouth. For you will be a witness for him to all men of what you have seen and heard. Now why do you wait? Arise, be baptized, and wash away your sins, calling on the name of the Lord.'

Acts 22:6-16 WEB

WEEK 13
Prophets and Apostles in the Redemption PLAN

He who angers you, controls you!

DATES

_____ TO _____

Monday
Prophets of God

Prophets were spokesmen for God. True prophets actually had God's words in their mouths. This is verbal inspiration. In both Old Testament and New Testament men and women were endowed by God supernaturally to speak for Him. It was a spiritual gift in the early church.

Tuesday
Apostles of Christ

Jesus chose twelve men to be His apostles and to supernaturally reveal God's Word. They were inspired to perform miracles. Judas betrayed Christ. Paul was added to the group "out of season." These men had the power to inspire others to perform miracles by laying on of hands.

Wednesday
Reveal the Truth

The work of the Holy Spirit was to reveal the truth of God's plan of redemption by inspiring the Apostles in two important ways: 1) by each of them being personal witnesses of Jesus, God's sacrifice for sin, and 2) by receiving the message of reconciliation and taking it to the entire world.

Thursday
Confirm the Word of God

The truth of God was confirmed by miracles, both by the Apostles and those on whom they laid their hands. The Old Testament Scriptures also provided evidence to the truth of the Gospel. The lasting product of their inspiration is the inerrant and eternal Scriptures, the Book of Truth.

Friday
In the Early Church

The Apostles, including Paul, went about establishing churches. Individuals in these churches were endued with miraculous gifts of the Holy Spirit. The truth of God was revealed by those who received the powers.

INSIDE TRACK

- [ ] 1 Corinthians 14:1-3
- [ ] 1 Corinthians 9:1-2
- [ ] John 15:26-27
- [ ] John 3:2
- [ ] 1 Corinthians 12:1-3

MIDDLE LANES

- [ ] Deuteronomy 18:14-22
- [ ] Jeremiah 31:27-34
- [ ]
- [ ] Matthew 10:1-41
- [ ] Luke 6:12-15
- [ ] Acts 9:1-22
- [ ] John 14:15-31
- [ ] Luke 24:36-49
- [ ] Matthew 28:18-20
- [ ] Acts 3:1-26
- [ ] Hebrews 2:1-4
- [ ]
- [ ] Acts 11:19-30
- [ ] Ephesians 3:1-13
- [ ] 1 Corinthians 14:1-25

FAST TRACK

- [ ] Judges 4:4-10
- [ ] 2 Kings 22:8-20
- [ ] Joel 2:28-32
- [ ] Acts 2:14-21
- [ ] Acts 21:7-14
- [ ] 1 Corinthians 15:1-11
- [ ] John 17:6-19
- [ ] John 13:21-30
- [ ] Mark 6:7-12
- [ ] Acts 8:14-25
- [ ] Acts 1:15-26
- [ ] John 2:15-19
- [ ] Philippians 2:5-11
- [ ] Acts 10:34-43
- [ ] Acts 11:15-18
- [ ] Acts 6:1-10
- [ ] 1 Timothy 4:6-16
- [ ] Hebrews 11:32-40
- [ ] Matthew 23:29-38
- [ ] Acts 7:35-53
- [ ] 1 Corinthians 12:4-31
- [ ] Galatians 3:16-29
- [ ] 1 Thessalonians 5:12-22
- [ ] Romans 16:1-16
- [ ] Ephesians 3:14-20

YOUR STORY...

At 13 years of age, the encouragement of friends helped Carol overcome her shyness long enough to respond to the gospel invitation. While she had been contemplating baptism for a couple of years, it was only after one friend went forward and another encouraged her to follow, that Carol was able to take that life-altering step.

Her home church building had no baptismal pool, so she, and her friends, traveled about five miles to a nearby church to be baptized by their minister, Bill Demombreun. Most of the members of her home congregation drove the five miles to witness the baptisms.

Carol's decision to become a child of God and her commitment to live for Him, had a profound impact on the course of her life. Her commitment to Christ prompted Carol to further her education at two Christian colleges and later, to contribute to the Christian education of others by teaching at Georgia Christian School in Dasher.

"Having a Christian husband and family, and coming to Georgia to teach at GCS [are the greatest blessings]. Otherwise, I do not know where I would be. The Christian life is the best way to live on earth, and heaven will be my final resting place," Carol said. "Nothing better!"

~Carol, 72

Growing Panes

No. 7-013

WEEK 14
The Redemptive Process "In Christ"

God teaches us to love by putting some unlovely people around us.

DATES
_____ TO _____

Monday
Faith

To believe in a fact is to believe that it really occurred; but to believe in Christ is to believe that he existed and to put our trust in him for our wisdom, justification, sanctification and redemption. We believe, not just with our intellects, but with our hearts.

Tuesday
Repentance

Repentance means "a change of mind." It includes a new view of Christ, sin and holiness. It is a change of understanding, a change of heart, a change of the will and a change of conduct. These changes produce a godly sorrow. Repentance is the difficult part of God's plan.

Wednesday
Confess Christ

The good confession made by Peter is the fundamental truth of the entire Bible. Jesus was to build his church on the truth that he is himself the promised Messiah, the Son of the living God. Those who would become members of His church were required to make this confession.

Thursday
Baptism

Baptism is for the remission of sins. It is a symbolic burial by immersion. Baptism typifies the death, burial and resurrection of Jesus. Baptism is the transfer point between the kingdom of darkness and sin and the kingdom of God. It is also the point where we begin a new life in Christ.

Friday
Walking in the Light

Christians may now go free from sin and enjoy the highest honors on the condition that you confess your faults, repent and walk in the light. Mercy and truth have come together...

INSIDE TRACK	MIDDLE LANES	FAST TRACK
John 3:16	Romans 10:1-17	Hebrews 11:1-40
	James 2:14-26	Genesis 22:1-18
	Acts 16:16-34	Joshua 2:1-21
		Isaiah 53:1-12
		John 20:24-29
Matthew 4:17	Luke 13:1-9	Luke 15:11-24
	Acts 2:38-39	Acts 8:14-24
	Acts 17:16-33	Matthew 21:28-32
		Luke 24:44-47
		Titus 2:11-14
Matthew 16:15-16	Luke 12:1-12	Matthew 26:69-75
	Philippians 2:1-11	Acts 8:27-39
		John 10:22-39
		Isaiah 45:20-25
		Acts 2:22-31
1 Peter 3:21	Romans 6:1-17	Hebrews 9:11-14
	Colossians 2:6-15	John 3:1-8
	Matthew 28:18-20	Acts 10:44-48
		Acts 19:1-7
		1 Corinthians 1:11-17
		Romans 13:1-14
Hebrews 10:35-36	1 John 1:5-10	Ephesians 4:1-22
	Romans 6:15-23	Ephesians 5:1-17
	Romans 12:1-21	Colossians 3:1-17
		Revelation 3:7-13

THE PLAN OF SALVATION

There are two parts to our Plan of Salvation, [1]God's part and [2]man's part.

Jesus, the Word that became flesh, was the sacrificial Lamb God provided as His part in this salvation covenant. The benefits of that salvation are given freely by the Grace of God. We neither deserved salvation nor could we ever do enough to earn it (Ephesians 2:8). We are saved by the Grace of God. Yet, a sacrifice was demanded and God provided it.

But man's part in the plan is also demanding. If you hope to spend eternity with God in heaven, you must "work out your own salvation with fear and trembling (Philippians 2:12)."

Thus, we understand that it is our own responsibility to answer the question, "What must I do to be saved?" by faithful obedience to God's instructions.

Man's part in the salvation plan is sacrificial faith. Because, "Not everyone who says to me, 'Lord, Lord,' will enter the kingdom of heaven, but only the one who does the will of my Father who is in heaven (Matthew 7:21).

The ultimate Gospel story is told like this: "I have been crucified with Christ and I no longer live, but Christ lives in me. The life that I now live in the body, I live by faith in the Son of God, who loved me and gave himself for me (Galatians 2:20-21)."

Growing Panes
No. 7-014

WEEK 15
The Church: Fellowship of the Saved

Quit griping about your church; if it was perfect, you couldn't belong.

DATES

_____ TO _____

Monday
The Kingdom of God

Christ reigns as King of Kings since his coronation. The Apostles were given the keys to the kingdom, the Word of God. Both Jesus and the Apostles said "the Kingdom of Heaven is at hand." On Pentecost Peter proclaimed that Jesus had been made Lord and Christ."

Tuesday
The Church and the Kingdom

The "redeemed ones" are called the Kingdom of God and the Church of God. Saints comprise the Kingdom of Jesus Christ and the Church of Christ. Christians are members of the Body of Christ. The church is the same as the Kingdom of God's Dear Son.

Wednesday
Christ, Our Shepherd/Head/Lord

Jesus is the loving Shepherd who cares for His sheep. He is the Head of the Body of Christ and we are members. Different members have different functions. Jesus the Christ is our Lord and Master. We are the same as bondservants because we have been bought with a price.

Thursday
Spiritual Blessings "in Christ"

Being in Christ means that the blood of Christ is available to us. Thus, forgiveness of sins is a principal blessing Christians enjoy being in Christ. Confidence in praying is also granted. After death, Christians have hope of life eternal with God because we are part of His Body.

Friday
Redemption "in Christ"

Therefore, Christians are redeemed from the bondage of past sins and enjoy the hope of a final redemption when Christ returns again. Then, we will be taken up to live with Him eternally.

INSIDE TRACK	MIDDLE LANES	FAST TRACK
Revelation 19:6	Daniel 2:1-48	Deuteronomy 10:12-22
	Isaiah 2:1-5	Psalm 24:1-10
	Matthew 3:1-3; 4:12-17	Psalm 118:19-24
		1 Timothy 6:11-16
		Hebrews 2: 5-9
Romans 16:16	Matthew 16:13-20	Job 19:23-29
	Acts 2:1-47	Acts 1:1-5
	Colossians 1:9-14	Ephesians 2:11-22
		Hebrews 9:15-22
		1 Peter 1:17-21
Isaiah 40:11	Colossians 1:15-19	Psalm 23:1-6
	Revelation 1:9-20	John 10:11-48
	1 Corinthians 12:12-30	1 Corinthians 6:12-20
		1 Corinthians 7:17-24
		Ephesians 5:22-32
James 5:16	Ephesians 1:3-23	2 Chronicles 7:12-18
	Ephesians 3:2-19	Matthew 7:7-11
		Acts 10:34-43
		Philippians 4:4-9
		1 John 1:5-10
John 14:1-3	Romans 3:21-26	Matthew 24:42-44
	Romans 6:1-14	Matthew 25:31-46
	Galatians 3:13-29	Luke 21:25-28
		1 Corinthians 15:50-57
		Hebrews 9:11-14

YOUR STORY...

You are never too old to change the direction of your life. John changed direction when he was baptized at the age of 57. He had been studying the Bible and was ready to change his life. His wife and his in-laws influenced him to become a Christian by their examples and through the teaching of scripture.

"I made the decision to make a change in the direction my life was unfolding. It is never too late," John said. Since that time, John has become *"more spiritually oriented and less worldly oriented"* as he learns to *"live life as a Christian."* His greatest blessing as a Christian, he said, is the forgiveness of his sins and the promise of eternal life if he remains faithful.

One way that John has learned to "live life as a Christian" is through formal study of God's Word. A 2016 graduate of Georgia School of Preaching and Biblical Studies, John often spends time in the pulpit preaching the good news he has been taught, and encouraging others to make whatever changes are necessary to ensure salvation.

"I felt relief and peace getting right with God by obeying the Gospel and [I have] been touched by the Holy Spirit ever since," he said. *"Being a Christian is a design for living life with much less negative consequences and is [the] platform for those heaven bound . . . "*

~John, 68

Growing Panes

No. 7-015

WEEK 16
Redemptive Leadership "In Christ"

DATES

_____ TO _____

Don't wait for 6 strong men to take you to church.

Monday
Christ, Our Example

Example is "stronger than precept" is a true maxim. Jesus alone is worthy to be our true religious model. Of all the Biblical models, Jesus was the only one who was tempted in all respects as we are, and yet without sin. His Father recognized Him as the only true Son of God.

Tuesday
Preachers and Teachers to Instruct

Preachers and teachers must hold fast the faithful word by both precept and example. Sound teaching both edifies the saved and convicts the gainsayers. Young disciples need the milk of the Word, while more mature servants must hear to maintain faithfulness.

Wednesday
Elders to Oversee

Elders signify the wisdom and experience in the faith. Overseers, or Bishops refer to leaders of authority in the task of watchful oversight of a congregation of God's children. Pastors, or Shepherds, describe the passionate concern for the sheep of God's pasture.

Thursday
Deacons to Serve

A deacon is a waiter, attendant, minister, or a special servant in the Lord's Church. While supervising the relief for the needy, they must be qualified to settle quarrels that may arise in the process. The deacons in the first century church attended to the secular concerns of the church.

Friday
Disciples of Christ

Christians use the power of their influence to effect change in others. We are followers of Christ. Faithful disciples go teach others to be faithful disciples as members of the Body of Christ in our world.

INSIDE TRACK	MIDDLE LANES	FAST TRACK
☐ Romans 5:1-2	☐ 1 Peter 2:11-21	☐ 1 Peter 3:8-12
	☐ 1 Timothy 4:1-16	☐ Isaiah 40:28-31
	☐ Hebrews 12:1-12	☐ 1 Peter 3:13-18
		☐ Philippians 3:12-16
		☐ James 1:2-8
☐ Matthew 7:28-29	☐ Titus 2:1-15	☐ Ephesians 4:9-16
	☐ James 3:1-18	☐ Hebrews 5:7-14
	☐ Matthew 7:15-29	☐ Hebrews 6:1-3
		☐ Romans 15:14-22
		☐
☐ Acts 20:28	☐ 1 Peter 5:1-4	☐ Titus 1:5-9
	☐ 1 Timothy 3:1-7	☐ John 10:1-18
	☐ Acts 20:17-31	☐ Ezekiel 34:1-10
		☐ Philippians 2:5-11
		☐ Acts 14:21-25
☐ Acts 6:3-4	☐ Acts 6:1-7	☐ Romans 12:3-8
	☐ 1 Timothy 3:8-13	☐ 2 Corinthians 9:9-15
	☐	☐ 1 Peter 4:7-11
		☐ 1 Timothy 5:3-8
		☐
	☐ 1 Corinthians 11:1	☐ Matthew 28:16-20
☐ John 8:31-32	☐ Matthew 4:18-22	☐ Colossians 2:9-12
	☐ Luke 9:57-62	☐ 1 Corinthians 12:27-31
		☐ 1 Corinthians 3:5-9
		☐ Mark 16:15-20

YOUR STORY...

Taking turns attending each other's church of origin seemed to be a perfectly acceptable and fair compromise. One Sunday at Lisa's church and the next Sunday at her husband's church. That became the agreement. But over time, something shifted.

Lisa had been studying the Bible more, and she began to "feel very at home" at her husband's church. Now expecting their first child, Lisa knew she did not want to raise her children in a house divided. *"I had prayed about it,"* Lisa said, *"and I knew it was time. I wanted my child to be raised by two Christian parents."* At 27 years old and eight months pregnant, Lisa was baptized into Christ. Fervent prayer, her husband's love, a friendly, welcoming church – all get credit for Lisa's conversion and all continue to fortify her faith. Raising her

boys in a Christian home has proven to be her greatest blessing this side of heaven, she said, and prayer has proven to be a powerful partner.

"My life has changed in many ways. I have a living and positive hope. I look at life situations differently now. I pray about everything, and I know the Lord hears my prayers and will always do what is best in my life."

Lisa acknowledged that life has not always been easy. The road has had many bumps and curves, she said, *"but God has always been present"* in her life, spurring her on, urging faithfulness. *"God is a loving God, and accepts us for who we are at the time we accept Him. He wants us to be with Him in heaven one day."*
~Lisa, 57

Growing Panes
No. 7-016

Commands to be Obeyed...

BE BAPTIZED INTO CHRIST

A Command of Jesus

Matthew 28:19-20 ESV

Go therefore and make disciples of all nations, baptizing them in the name of the Father and of the Son and of the Holy Spirit, teaching them to observe all that I have commanded you. And behold, I am with you always, to the end of the age."

Proclaimed by Apostles

Acts 22:16 ESV

And now why do you wait? Rise and be baptized and wash away your sins, calling on his name.

Romans 6:3-7 ESV

Do you not know that all of us who have been baptized into Christ Jesus were baptized into his death? We were buried therefore with him by baptism into death, in order that, just as Christ was raised from the dead by the glory of the Father, we too might walk in newness of life. For if we have been united with him in a death like his, we shall certainly be united with him in a resurrection like his. We know that our old self was crucified with him in order that the body of sin might be brought to nothing, so that we would no longer be enslaved to sin. For one who has died has been set free from sin.

Galatians 3:27 ESV

For as many of you as were baptized into Christ have put on Christ.

1 Peter 3:21-22 ESV

Baptism, which corresponds to this, now saves you, not as a removal of dirt from the body but as an appeal to God for a good conscience, through the resurrection of Jesus Christ, who has gone into heaven and is at the right hand of God, with angels, authorities, and powers having been subjected to him.

Colossians 2:11-13 ESV

In him also you were circumcised with a circumcision made without hands, by putting off the body of the flesh, by the circumcision of Christ, having been buried with him in baptism, in which you were also raised with him through faith in the powerful working of God, who raised him from the dead. And you, who were dead in your trespasses and the uncircumcision of your flesh, God made alive together with him, having forgiven us all our trespasses,

For Forgiveness of Sins

Acts 2:38 ESV

And Peter said to them, "Repent and be baptized every one of you in the name of Jesus Christ for the forgiveness of your sins, and you will receive the gift of the Holy Spirit.

Gentiles Hear the Good News

Peter opened his mouth and said, "Truly I perceive that God doesn't show favoritism; but in every nation he who fears him and works righteousness is acceptable to him. The word which he sent to the children of Israel, preaching good news of peace by Jesus Christ—he is Lord of all— you yourselves know what happened, which was proclaimed throughout all Judea, beginning from Galilee, after the baptism which John preached; even Jesus of Nazareth, how God anointed him with the Holy Spirit and with power, who went about doing good and healing all who were oppressed by the devil, for God was with him. We are witnesses of everything he did both in the country of the Jews, and in Jerusalem; whom they also killed, hanging him on a tree. God raised him up the third day, and gave him to be revealed, not to all the people, but to witnesses who were chosen before by God, to us, who ate and drank with him after he rose from the dead. He commanded us to preach to the people and to testify that this is he who is appointed by God as the Judge of the living and the dead. All the prophets testify about him, that through his name everyone who believes in him will receive remission of sins."

While Peter was still speaking these words, the Holy Spirit fell on all those who heard the word. They of the circumcision who believed were amazed, as many as came with Peter, because the gift of the Holy Spirit was also poured out on the Gentiles. For they heard them speaking in other languages and magnifying God. Then Peter answered, "Can any man forbid the water, that these who have received the Holy Spirit as well as we should not be baptized?" He commanded them to be baptized in the name of Jesus Christ. Then they asked him to stay some days.

- Acts 10:34-48 WEB

WEEK 17
Preaching the Message of Redemption

It is easier to preach ten sermons than it is to live one.

DATES

_____ TO _____

Monday
Evangelizing the Lost World

God's will and purpose is to save all who will call on him in sincerity and truth. The early disciples went everywhere preaching the Word. By Divine appointment the church has been given the mission of converting the world by preaching the Gospel.

Tuesday
The Gospel is for All

Preaching is to convince the world that Jesus Christ is the Son of God and to persuade all nations to receive, honor, love, serve and obey him. The Book of Acts is a history of how the early church evangelized their world. The power to save was placed in "earthen vessels."

Wednesday
Individuals Teaching Individuals

The Great Commission was given to the Twelve to "go into all the world" preaching he Gospel. Every disciple is charged with the task of teaching others. The New Testament church, composed of individual Christians, is the pillar and support of the Truth.

Thursday
Churches Sending Missionaries

Thus, the churches in Jerusalem and Antioch evangelized the world by sending preachers to all the parts of their world. Their mission was to preach, baptize and make disciples of Jesus. They also were charged with teaching the converts to obey all the teachings of Christ.

Friday
Churches Cooperating Together

Congregations cooperated with other congregations by sharing information, providing personnel and by giving financial support. The Body of Christ is one, with many congregations of saints.

INSIDE TRACK	MIDDLE LANES	FAST TRACK
☐ 2 Peter 3:9	☐ Mark 16:9-20	☐ Romans 1:8-17
	☐ 2 Corinthians 5:11-21	☐ 1 Peter 1:1-12
	☐ Revelation 22:12-21	☐ 1 Timothy 2:1-7
		☐ Romans 10:1-21
		☐ Titus 3:3-8
☐ 2 Timothy 4:2	☐ Acts 10:9-11:18	☐ Acts 16:6-15
	☐ Acts 13:1-52	☐ Acts 17:1-4
	☐	☐ 1 Corinthians 1:17-2:5
		☐ 2 Corinthians 4:1-15
		☐ Ephesians 3:1-13
☐ 1 Timothy 3:15	☐ Acts 9:1-19	☐ Matthew 28:16-20
	☐ Acts 8:1-40	☐ Acts 16:16-34
	☐	☐ Acts 18:24-26
		☐ 2 Timothy 4:1-5
		☐ Acts 2:42-47
☐ 1 Peter 2:9	☐ Acts 14:1-28	☐ Acts 15:22-35
	☐	☐ Acts 15:36-41
	☐	☐ Acts 20:13-38
		☐ 2 Corinthians 2:12-3:6
		☐ Ephesians 4:11-16
☐ Romans 12:4-5	☐ 1 Corinthians 16:1-18	☐ Romans 16:1-16
	☐ 2 Corinthians 8:1-24	☐ 2 Corinthians 9:1-15
	☐	☐ Colossians 4:7-18
		☐ 1 Corinthians 12:12-27
		☐

YOUR STORY...

First, a "We Do" to Christ; then, an "I do" to each other. Craig and Kate grew up in Christian homes, attended church services regularly, and always endeavored to make sound, well-thought-out decisions. As their relationship grew and deepened, and plans for their future together began to take shape, careful consideration was given to their relationship with God. Oneness with Christ would be key to a successful marriage, they reasoned together.

"We knew we wanted to put God first in our new marriage, for ourselves, and our future children. We wanted to provide a good Christian home for our family." The week before their wedding, Craig and Kate were baptized. *"It was an incredible experience being baptized together, then a week later, being married in the same spot in front of friends and family."*

Being unified in Christ keeps Craig and Kate unified in their marriage, they said. They strengthen their shared faith and safeguard their marriage covenant with daily prayer and devotional together. Putting God first inspires them to put each other first. Craig and Kate strive to exemplify the royal law of love – respect, mercy and kindness – both in and out of the home, influencing others for good and glorifying God.

"We want others to see us and know we love the Lord and each other."

~Kate, 20s/Craig, 30s

Growing Panes

No. 7-017

WEEK 18
Worship Praise to Our Redeemer

DATES

_____ TO _____

Be ye fishers of men. You catch 'em - He'll clean 'em.

Monday
Glory to God in the Highest

From the beginning of time praise has been commonly associated with prayer as a part of our worship of Jehovah. At the birth of Jesus men on earth and the angels in heaven gave glory and honor to our God. Worship is a vital part of our walk with Jesus as Christians.

Tuesday
False Worship

Idol worship is testimony to man's universal need to worship, even if it is false. Even very religious worshippers like the Pharisees may engage in worship that is void. False worship focuses on the creation rather than the Creator. It rejects God's wisdom and establishes its own.

Wednesday
Worship in Spirit and Truth

True worship involves the proper attitude and the proper practices. God must be worshipped in the way He has instructed. God teaches his disciples how, when, and by what actions he is to be worshipped. True worshippers act upon their faith, which is based on these teachings of God.

Thursday
Prayer

The blessing of petitioning Almighty God is a gracious provision of God's Scheme of Redemption. God's children are encouraged to pray; to pray always; to pray anywhere; to pray for anything. Prayer also cultivates our spiritual nature and enables a close relationship with God.

Friday
Praise

Christians teach and admonish each other as they sing psalms, hymns and spiritual songs in worship to God. Singing is an act of worship in which melody is played on the strings of the heart. God is praised.

INSIDE TRACK	MIDDLE LANES	FAST TRACK
☐ Luke 2:13-14	☐ Psalm 42:1-11	☐ Psalm 63:1-11
	☐ Psalm 47:1-9	☐ Isaiah 26:1-21
	☐ Luke 2:1-15	☐ Isaiah 9:6-7
		☐ Revelation 4:1-11
		☐ Hebrews 9:1-16
☐ Acts 17:24	☐ Leviticus 10:1-3	☐ 1 Corinthians 14:26-39
	☐ Matthew 15:1-9	☐ 1 Kings 18:16-29
	☐ Acts 17:22-31	☐ Matthew 23:16-22
		☐ Colossians 2:16-23
		☐
☐ Ephesians 2:22	☐ John 4:1-26	☐ Isaiah 1:10-20
	☐ Ephesians 2:19-22	☐ 1 Corinthians 3:10-23
	☐	☐ Philippians 3:2-3
		☐
		☐
☐ John 4:23	☐ Romans 2:1-11	☐ John 17:6-19
	☐ Deuteronomy 5:23-33	☐ 2 Corinthians 13:1-10
	☐ 1 John 2:3-6	☐ 3 John 1:1-4
		☐ Joshua 24:13-15
		☐
☐ Colossians 3:16	☐ Hebrews 2:5-12	☐ Acts 16:22-29
	☐ Ephesians 5:15-20	☐ Romans 15:5-9
	☐ Colossians 3:15-17	☐ 1 Corinthians 14:13-19
		☐ Revelation 7:9-12
		☐

YOUR STORY...

On Monday, August 7, 2017, with family members as witnesses, Josiah's father baptized him in a spring-fed creek near their rural home. Summer was at its peak, but the water was freezing, and *"I didn't stay in it long."*

Eleven-year-old Josiah knew that being *"fixed on Jesus"* was how he wanted to live his life. *"I knew I would be making a commitment to Jesus. If I was a Christian, I would know that I was fixed on Jesus, and I would take that seriously, and be a better person,"* Josiah said.

While no one person influenced his decision to become a Christian, Josiah said, he does have a "top 5" list. *"Mom and Dad, of course, were great role models to me, so they are pretty high on the list."* Bible schoolteachers round out his top

5. Josiah refers to one as *"a great teacher;"* another as *"very spiritually encouraging."* A third teacher persuaded with her *"kind, joyous, Christian spirit."*

Josiah finds comfort in the assurance that so long as he remains fixed on Jesus, he is heaven bound. *"I know I still sin, but he forgives me,"* Josiah said. *"I also know that I'm going to have to spread the word about Jesus and I just don't know how since I'm not very good at talking to people."*

And yet, he confidently begins with this:
"Without Jesus, it's useless. You could be very generous; you could be very willing to do things for other people, but without Jesus . . . you really get nowhere. With Jesus, you can be perfected."
~Josiah, 12

Growing Panes

No. 7-018

WEEK 19
The Lord's Day and Giving

DATES

_____ TO _____

The Will of God will never take you to where the Grace of God will not protect you.

Monday
Christ Arose: First Day of the Week

On the first day of the week Christ arose from the dead and brought life and immortality to light for a lost world. The message of the Bible hangs on the resurrection of Jesus on the first day of the week. This day can rightly be called "the Lord's Day" because of His victory over death.

Tuesday
Met with His Disciples: First Day of the Week

On two occasions between His resurrection and His ascension, when the disciples of Jesus were assembled together, Christ met with them. They came together on Sunday, the first day of the week. When Jesus met with them, He blessed them.

Wednesday
Church Began: First Day of the Week

The church of Christ began on the day of Pentecost, which always fell on a Sunday. This was an event in prophecy. The Apostles received the miraculous gift of the Holy Spirit to deliver the soul-saving gospel for the first time. Three thousand accepted it, believed it and obeyed it.

Thursday
Early Church Met: First Day of the Week

The early church gathered together on Sundays to edify each other and to glorify God in worship. By the end of the first century, that day was called "the Lord's Day." The Lord's Day became a special day. Christians were urged to not forsake it, but to honor God on that day.

Friday
Our Giving: First Day of the Week

Several acts of worship were the focus of the Lord's Day gatherings in the New Testament, including giving. The Scriptures teach that we honor God when we give to others' needs.

INSIDE TRACK	MIDDLE LANES	FAST TRACK
☐ Matthew 16:21	☐ John 20:1-10	☐ Mark 16:1-8
	☐ Matthew 28:1-10	☐ Luke 18:31-39
	☐ Luke 24:1-12	☐ Isaiah 53:1-12
		☐ Acts 13:26-41
		☐ 1 Peter 2:4-10
☐ John 14:1-2	☐ John 20:19-29	☐ Luke 24:36-49
	☐	☐ John 14:23-31
	☐	☐ John 16:12-16
		☐ Matthew 28:16-20
		☐ Numbers 6:22-27
☐ Acts 20:16	☐ Acts 2:1-41	☐ Numbers 28:26-31
	☐ Leviticus 23:9-21	☐ 1 Corinthians 16:8
	☐ Acts 11:1-18	☐ Joel 2:28-32
		☐ Acts 10:34-48
		☐
☐ Hebrews 12:28-29	☐ Acts 20:7-12	☐ Romans 15:1-6
	☐ Revelation 1:9-11	☐ Psalm 89:1-16
	☐ Hebrews 10:19-25	☐ Romans 14:9-12
		☐ Romans 12:1-8
		☐ Titus 2:11-14
☐ Acts 20:34-35	☐ 1 Corinthians 16:1-4	☐ Matthew 6:1-4
	☐ 2 Corinthians 8:1-15	☐ 1 Chronicles 29:10-19
	☐ 2 Corinthians 9:1-15	☐ Proverbs 19:17
		☐ Matthew 25:31-46
		☐ Acts 9:36-43

YOUR STORY...

Steadfast faith – faith firmly rooted in God's word, and daily refreshed and strengthened by God's promises – diminishes the burdens and worries of this world.

For 40 years, Danny knew "about being a Christian." Danny's mother had a powerful influence on his life and his beliefs, Danny said, as she taught him about the promises of God.

But it was three year ago, at the age of forty-eight, that Bible knowledge and Christian influence united to pierce his heart, convict his soul, and lead him to baptism.

"I know where I am going . . . Heaven is my home." God's promises are true, and He brings joy and peace, Danny said. God has great things in store for all of us, Danny said, if we let Him work in our lives.

"You don't have to die, you can live forever. There is no greater love than His. He sacrificed His life so we can be free. We don't have to live in bondage because He broke those chains and shackles on Calvary over two thousand years ago.

You won't be the same ever again."

~Danny, 51

Growing Panes

No. 7-019

WEEK 20
Lord's Supper: Remembering Our Redeemer

DATES

_____ TO _____

Come as you are. You can change inside.

Monday
Passover Feast Memorial

The night before Jesus gave himself as a sin-offering on the cross, at the Passover, He instituted the Lord's Supper. The primary purpose was to keep ever fresh in our minds the first great fact of the Gospel: *"that Christ died for our sins according to the Scriptures."*

Tuesday
A Memorial Proclamation

The supper is commemorative, but more it is a proclamation of the fact that Jesus lives and will come again to collect his own to live with him eternally. Not only do we look back, but we look forward. Eating the bread and drinking from the cup nourishes the souls of the redeemed.

Wednesday
The Bread of Life

The bread is the symbolic body of Christ. Our unity in the Body of Christ is our focus when we eat together. We offer our bodies as *living sacrifices* as we remember how Christ gave his body as a sacrifice for our sins. Jesus said we are to eat his (symbolic) flesh.

Thursday
The Redeeming Blood

Likewise, Christians drink of the cup representative of the blood of Christ. Blood sacrifice was always associated with life-giving redemption. Every Lord's Day when Christians observe the Lord's Supper we proclaim the redemptive power of the blood of Christ.

Friday
Requires Self-Examination

Finally, the Lord's Supper is a time for self-examination...to see ourselves as God sees us; to test the attitudes of our minds against the actions in our lives. Here we personally face God.

INSIDE TRACK	MIDDLE LANES	FAST TRACK
☐ Matthew 26:2	☐ Matthew 26:17-30	☐ Mark 14:12-25
	☐ Exodus 12:1-30	☐ Mark 8:31-38
	☐ Hebrews 11:24-28	☐ Isaiah 53:1-12
		☐ 1 Peter 2:23-25
		☐
☐ Revelation 1:18	☐ 1 Corinthians 11:20-26	☐ John 14:1-6
	☐ 1 Thess. 4:13-18	☐ Romans 8:31-39
	☐ Revelation 1:4-8	☐ 1 Corinthians 15:20-28
		☐ 1 Corinthians 15:50-57
		☐ Matthew 16:24-27
☐ Romans 6:13	☐ Luke 22:7-23	☐ Ephesians 5:1-2
	☐ John 6:25-59	☐ Hebrews 13:15-16
	☐	☐ 1 Corinthians 6:19-20
		☐ 1 Peter 2:4-10
		☐ Romans 12:1-2
☐ Leviticus 17:11	☐ 1 Corinthians 10:14-17	☐ Ephesians 1:3-10
	☐ Hebrews 9:11-28	☐ Hebrews 10:19-25
	☐	☐ Colossians 1:13-20
		☐ Romans 3:21-26
		☐ 1 John 5:5-12
☐ Psalm 26:2	☐ 1 Corinthians 11:27-32	☐ Hebrews 12:1-3
	☐ 2 Corinthians 13:5-10	☐ 1 Corinthians 5:6-8
	☐ Galatians 6:1-6	☐ Romans 14:9-12
		☐ Colossians 3:12-17
		☐ Philippians 2:1-18

YOUR STORY...

Sammie Pope was unable to move, virtually paralyzed from the neck down, yet after his baptism, he taught many people about Christ.

In the late 1950s, Sammie and his widowed mother began studying the Bible with members of the church. During those studies, Sammie confessed Jesus as Lord and expressed his desire to be baptized in obedience to the Gospel. Men of the church leaped into action, fashioning a cot for Sammie out of pipe and 1 x 1s. He was transported via station wagon to Loch Laurel lake to be baptized.

At the lake, the men carried Sammie on the cot down the hill to the water. While his mother held his nose, Sammie was immersed and added to the kingdom of Christ. Sammie's mother was baptized immediately after, as Sammie proudly looked on.

Over the remainder of his life, Sammie loved having the Bible regularly read to him. His disabilities left him unable to do most things, but Sammie was able – and eager – to share the gospel with others. Sammie was determined to do the something that he could. It is believed that Sammie taught nine or ten people about Christ in the ten or so years before his death.

~Submitted by MP

Growing Panes

No. 7-020

Commands to be Obeyed...

REMAIN FAITHFUL TO CHRIST

Grow Spiritually

Ephesians 4:14-24 NIV

Then we will no longer be infants, tossed back and forth by the waves, and blown here and there by every wind of teaching and by the cunning and craftiness of people in their deceitful scheming. Instead, speaking the truth in love, we will grow to become in every respect the mature body of him who is the head, that is, Christ. From him the whole body, joined and held together by every supporting ligament, grows and builds itself up in love, as each part does its work.

So I tell you this, and insist on it in the Lord, that you must no longer live as the Gentiles do, in the futility of their thinking. They are darkened in their understanding and separated from the life of God because of the ignorance that is in them due to the hardening of their hearts. Having lost all sensitivity, they have given themselves over to sensuality so as to indulge in every kind of impurity, and they are full of greed.

That, however, is not the way of life you learned when you heard about Christ and were taught in him in accordance with the truth that is in Jesus. You were taught, with regard to your former way of life, to put off your old self, which is being corrupted by its deceitful desires; to be made new in the attitude of your minds; and to put on the new self, created to be like God in true righteousness and holiness.

2 Peter 1:5-11 NIV

For this very reason, make every effort to supplement your faith with virtue, and virtue with knowledge, and knowledge with self-control, and self-control with steadfastness, and steadfastness with godliness, and godliness with brotherly affection, and brotherly affection with love. For if these qualities are yours and are increasing, they keep you from being ineffective or unfruitful in the knowledge of our Lord Jesus Christ. For whoever lacks these qualities is so nearsighted that he is blind, having forgotten that he was cleansed from his former sins.

Therefore, brothers, be all the more diligent to confirm your calling and election, for if you practice these qualities you will never fall. For in this way there will be richly provided for you an entrance into the eternal kingdom of our Lord and Savior Jesus Christ.

Observe the Great Commission

Matthew 28:16-20 ESV

Now the eleven disciples went to Galilee, to the mountain to which Jesus had directed them. And when they saw him they worshiped him, but some doubted.

And Jesus came and said to them, "All authority in heaven and on earth has been given to me. Go therefore and make disciples of all nations, baptizing them in[b] the name of the Father and of the Son and of the Holy Spirit, teaching them to observe all that I have commanded you. And behold, I am with you always, to the end of the age."

Lydia is Converted to Christ

Setting sail therefore from Troas, we made a straight course to Samothrace, and the day following to Neapolis; and from there to Philippi, which is a city of Macedonia, the foremost of the district, a Roman colony. We were staying some days in this city. On the Sabbath day we went forth outside of the city by a riverside, where we supposed there was a place of prayer, and we sat down, and spoke to the women who had come together.

A certain woman named Lydia, a seller of purple, of the city of Thyatira, one who worshiped God, heard us; whose heart the Lord opened to listen to the things which were spoken by Paul. When she and her household were baptized, she begged us, saying, "If you have judged me to be faithful to the Lord, come into my house, and stay." So she persuaded us.

(Acts 16:11-15 WEB).

The Corinthians Obey the Gospel

Crispus, the ruler of the synagogue, believed in the Lord with all his house. Many of the Corinthians, when they heard, believed and were baptized. The Lord said to Paul in the night by a vision, "Don't be afraid, but speak and don't be silent; for I am with you, and no one will attack you to harm you, for I have many people in this city." He lived there a year and six months, teaching the word of God among them.

(Acts 18:8-10 WEB)

WEEK 21
Conditions of Church Membership

The love we have is God's gift to us; what we do with it is our gift to God.

DATES

_____ TO _____

Monday
Converted to Christ

Membership in the church of Christ is the result of being converted, born again. Disciples are followers of Jesus, forsaking all others. Christians have turned from (repented) of the dark things of the world to become the children of Light. We now live a new life in Christ.

Tuesday
Baptized into His Body

We were baptized into Christ (His Body, the church) for the remission of our sins. Through our baptism we became, by blood, the (spiritual faith) children of Light. In return, we give our bodies as a living sacrifice to God. Baptized believers continue to learn as His disciples.

Wednesday
Benefit from the Redeeming Blood

In Christ we are blessed with forgiveness of sins as we contact the redeeming blood of Christ. If we continue to "walk in the light" the redeeming blood of Jesus continues to cleanse us from sin. But, we are not our own, we have been bought with the price of His shed blood.

Thursday
Live a Life Faithful to Christ

Faithfully living for Jesus requires growing in the knowledge of His Will and faithful obedience in what pleases Him. Our life must bear the fruits of discipleship. Christians are the light of the world, and as such, must let their light shine.

Friday
Love God, Love People, Serve the World

God is love, and He loved us even while we were still sinners. The world will be convinced that we are His disciples when we show love for each other. Our love must be genuine, from the heart.

INSIDE TRACK	MIDDLE LANES	FAST TRACK
☐ John 14:6	☐ Matthew 18:1-35 ☐ Luke 14:25-35 ☐ John 3:1-21	☐ Mark 8:34-38 ☐ Acts 2:42 ☐ Acts 17:28-31 ☐ Acts 26:14-18 ☐ Ephesians 4:20-24
☐ Acts 22:16	☐ 1 Corinthians 12:12-31 ☐ Romans 12:1-20 ☐ Matthew 28:18-20	☐ Romans 6:1-7 ☐ 1 Peter 3:18-22 ☐ Hebrews 10:19-23 ☐ Acts 2:36-41 ☐ Acts 8:26-38
☐ Ephesians 1:7	☐ Ephesians 2:11-22 ☐ 1 John 1:5-10 ☐ 1 John 5:1-12	☐ Hebrews 9:11-15 ☐ Romans 3:21-26 ☐ 1 Peter 1:17-21 ☐ 1 Corinthians 6:18-20 ☐ Titus 2:11-14
☐ Hebrews 13:5	☐ Colossians 1:9-14 ☐ Matthew 5:1-48 ☐ Revelation 2:1-29	☐ Colossians 3:5-11 ☐ Colossians 4:2-6 ☐ Titus 2:1-8 ☐ James 1:19-27 ☐ John 15:5-8
☐ Deuteronomy 7:9	☐ 1 Corinthians 13:1-13 ☐ John 13:1-38 ☐ 1 Timothy 1:3-7	☐ 1 John 2:15-17 ☐ 1 John 3:16-20 ☐ Romans 5:1-8 ☐ Romans 13:8-10 ☐

Never too late!

After retiring from his job in the oil fields of New Orleans, Thurmond and his wife, Bluie, moved to Muskogee, Oklahoma to care for their aging mothers. Thurmond's mother was a strong faithful Christian who delighted in correcting others. Bluie brought her mother with her from New Orleans. Her mother was in her mid-nineties, bedridden and very frail.

Thurmond was at the church office every day because he volunteered to print the weekly bulletin and other needed Bible lessons. We talked a lot about the fact that Bluie's mother was not a Christian. She had never been baptized into Christ (Matthew 28:18-20). We would discuss his most recent conversations with her as he attempted to teach her about Christ.

One day he came in and said "Granny wants to be baptized." She was very weak and totally bedfast. Weighing less than one hundred pounds, she looked more like a young girl than a 90-*plus*-year-old woman. We reviewed the problems of her being baptized, but concluded that we had to find a way to honor her wishes.

Later that day Granny was brought to the church building on a gurney. Thurmond, with the assistance of three other men, lowered her into the water on a clean white bedsheet.

That day, near her death, she confessed her faith in Jesus as the Christ and was baptized for the remission of her sins. –grh

Growing Panes

No. 7-021

WEEK 22
Serving the World

YOU are the only Bible some people may ever read.

Monday
By Setting a Good Example

Christianity is both *caught* and *taught*. They shine as *light* to guide and direct sinners to Christ; and when they come in contact with others they serve as *salt*. The power of our Christian influence affects others by our words, deeds and personal behaviors.

Tuesday
By Living the Redemption Story

Christians have been redeemed from the bondage to sin by the blood of Christ. Our testimony is that we are saved by grace for the purpose of doing good works. The length, width and depth of God's love motivates us to show the same kind of love to others.

Wednesday
By Being Faithful Members of the Church

As the Bride of Christ we are commanded to remain faithful to Him. His desire is to present us as a radiant church without spot or blemish, holy and blameless. Faithfulness will require courage, spiritual strength, and love. In addition, we must submit ourselves to our Lord.

Thursday
By Caring

Christians care for the widows, homeless children, the poor, those in prison, those who are physically sick, and any other person in need. Three things happen when we help others: someone is helped, we grow spiritually, and we are serving Christ.

Friday
By Loving

The two greatest commandments are for us to love God and to love our neighbor. The world can see that we are Christ's disciples if we love one another.

INSIDE TRACK	MIDDLE LANES	FAST TRACK
☐ Matthew 5:13-14	☐ 1 Timothy 4:1-16	☐ Matthew 5:13-16
	☐ 2 Peter 1:3-11	☐ Proverbs 4:1-27
	☐ Titus 2:1-15	☐ 1 Peter 2:21-25
		☐ John 13:12-17
		☐ Hebrews 6:9-12
☐ Ephesians 2:8-9	☐ Ephesians 3:1-21	☐ Ephesians 1:3-14
	☐ Ephesians 4:1-32	☐ Colossians 1:9-14
	☐ Ephesians 5:1-20	☐ Romans 3:21-26
		☐ 1 John 4:7-12
		☐
☐ Revelation 19:7-8	☐ Ephesians 5:21-33	☐ James 4:1-12
	☐ 1 Corinthians 16:5-24	☐ Ephesians 6:10-20
	☐	☐ 2 Timothy 1:6-12
		☐ Philippians 4:10-13
		☐ Galatians 2:19-21
☐ Galatians 6:2	☐ James 1:19-27	☐ 1 John 3:16-18
	☐ Acts 6:1-7	☐ Philippians 2:1-11
	☐	☐ Galatians 6:7-10
		☐ Hebrews 13:1-3
		☐ James 2:14-17
☐ Matthew 19:19	☐ Matthew 22:24-40	☐ Matthew 25:35-40
	☐ Luke 6:27-36	☐ Luke 10:25-37
	☐ John 13:34-35	☐ Mark 12:28-34
		☐ John 15:9-17
		☐ Romans 13:8-10

YOUR STORY...

Marie credits her conversion to Fred Shields, a deacon in the church, who asked Marie to participate in a Bible study. By her own account, Marie really didn't want to, but Fred was persistent. Marie acquiesced, and soon, this self-taught Bible scholar was giving Marie chapter and verse for every doctrinal question she had. The Jule Miller filmstrips were convincing, but it was his faithful Christian example that truly sealed the deal for her.

"His Christian example and knowledge of the Scriptures peaked my interest in Bible study and led me to question many doctrinal issues I had accepted in my childhood," Marie said. Marie's husband and his family also greatly influenced her decision, and she is convinced that their home would have been very different had she not become a Christian.

Marie now has answers to life's greatest questions, something she considers to be one of the greatest blessings of being a Christian. *"When you are a Christian,"* she said, *"you can say 'in everything give thanks.'"*

It is that Christian attitude that enables Marie to recognize another blessing from the past – a blessing that was difficult to accept as a young bride.

"After my baptism," she said, *"my husband began working long hours, and I was alone many nights. I spent the time studying the scriptures. I give thanks today for those lonely nights that enriched my faith!"*

~Marie, 70

Growing Panes
No. 7-022

WEEK 23
God's Love Reflected in His Disciples

Don't let the noise of the world drown out the peace of God's love.

DATES

_____ TO _____

INSIDE TRACK
- [ ] Mark 12:29-31
- [ ] Ephesians 6:23-24
- [ ] 2 Thessalonians 1:3
- [ ] Mark 10:21-22
- [ ] Luke 6:27-29

MIDDLE LANES
- [ ] 1 Corinthians 13:1-13
- [ ] James 2:1-17
- [ ]
- [ ] 1 John 5:1-12
- [ ] Romans 8:28-30
- [ ] John 14:15-24
- [ ] 1 John 2:3-11
- [ ] 1 John 4:7-21
- [ ] 1 Peter 4:1-11
- [ ] John 3:16-21
- [ ] Matthew 9:35-38
- [ ] 1 Corinthians 9:19-23
- [ ] Matthew 5:43-44
- [ ] Matthew 27:27-38
- [ ] Luke 6:35-36

FAST TRACK
- [ ] Mark 12:28-34
- [ ] John 13:1-5
- [ ] Ephesians 2:1-10
- [ ] Titus 3:3-8
- [ ] 1 John 3:1-18
- [ ] Matthew 10:32-39
- [ ] Matthew 22:37-40
- [ ] Luke 10:25-37
- [ ] Romans 8:37-39
- [ ] 2 Corinthians 5:14-15
- [ ] John 15:9-17
- [ ] Ephesians 1:15-17
- [ ] Colossians 1:3-8
- [ ] 1 Thessalonians 4:9-10
- [ ] 1 Peter 1:22-25
- [ ] John 17:20-23
- [ ] Romans 5:1-8
- [ ] Jude 1:17-23
- [ ] Philippians 2:1-11
- [ ] 1 Thessalonians 2:1-9
- [ ] Romans 12:9-21
- [ ] Romans 13:8-10
- [ ] Ephesians 4:14-16
- [ ] 2 Timothy 2:24-26
- [ ] 1 Peter 2:20-25

Monday
Love Defined

God is love. Any description of love must include the attributes of God. God's love included loving us even when we were sinners. God hates sin, but he loves the sinner. Three core principles of Christianity are faith, hope, and love. The greatest of these three is love.

Tuesday
Love God

Our love for God must supersede all other loves including our parents, children or ourselves. We are to love God above everything and everyone. Our love for God is shown by doing what He says in faithful obedience. Jesus is our model for how he loved His father.

Wednesday
Love Fellow Christians

Christians are commanded to love one another. In fact, all men will know we are disciples of Jesus by how we show love to each other. In addition, our love for our brothers and sisters in Christ is shown by how we respond to their physical and spiritual needs.

Thursday
Love the Lost

God so loved the lost world that he sent his one and only son. The greatest mystery of the Scheme of Redemption is how God loved us as sinners. God wants all mankind to be saved from sin. Christians are told to go into all the world preaching Christ so that sinners can be saved.

Friday
Love Our Enemies

Loving our enemies is, perhaps, the most difficult command. That's why we should not let the sun go down on our wrath. Jesus forgave those who killed him before they repented. True love for our enemies causes us to act quickly to forgive.

YOUR STORY...

While he attended church regularly, Jack questioned whether he was "good enough" to be a Christian.

Fifty-two years ago, after hearing a sermon about the second coming of Christ, Jack decided, "good enough" or not, he wanted to be ready when Christ returned. *"He (the minister) made a point that if you had not become a Christian before Christ came again, you would never have another chance . . . I wanted to be saved and not spend eternity in hell with all the lost,"* Jack recalls.

Jack faithfully attended church with his wife, so when he responded to the invitation on that Sunday, the minister was stumped. *". . . [he] thought I was already a Christian because I was present at all church functions . . ."* But Jack understood that simply hanging out with Christians did not make him a Christian, although his regular association with Christians, and the example of his Christian wife, definitely encouraged him to take the necessary steps.

Jack also began to realize that *"no one would ever be good enough"* to be a Christian, but an avenue of forgiveness and salvation was available *"if I repent...[be] baptized and have my sins forgiven."*

"I want to go to Heaven after this life is over," Jack said, *"and only Christians go to Heaven."*

~Jack, 85

Growing Panes
No.7-023

WEEK 24
The Peace that Passes Understanding

Don't tell God how big your storm is; tell the storm how big your God is!

DATES _____ TO _____

Monday
The Prince of Peace

Peace is inner tranquility, the absence of hostility. Both righteous disciples as well as the wicked need peace. The Prince of Peace shows us the way to peace by his humility and selfless service.

Tuesday
Peace with God

"No God, *no* peace! Know God, *know* peace!" Redemption by the blood of Christ leads to peace. Obedience to the Word of God, by faith, results in reconciliation with the God of Peace. God's peace is beyond description!

Wednesday
Peace with Your Brother

Brotherly love results in peace. When brethren disagree and harbor malice, our Gospel message will not be reinforced. Resolve, or lay aside the causes of contention, live in harmony. Maintain unity and avoid damaging division. Pursue peace.

Thursday
Congregational Peace

Peace and harmony prevail when we set our minds on things above. We are God's chosen people, holy and dearly loved. Love is what binds us together and makes for peace; whether in our families or the local congregation.

Friday
Dwelling Together in Peace

How we use our tongues is critical to maintaining peace. Some of the traits that control the tongue are: self-control, compassion, humility, and love. "Do not judge another" is a basic rule for dwelling together in peace.

INSIDE TRACK	MIDDLE LANES	FAST TRACK
Galatians 5:22	Luke 2:8-14	Isaiah 9:1-7
	John 14:23-27	Romans 12:14-21
	Romans 5:1-11	Psalm 85:7-13
		Galatians 5:13-17
		Luke 23:39-49
John 14:15	Isaiah 59:1-8	2 Corinthians 5:17-21
	Romans 5:1-11	1 Peter 1:3-23
	Hebrews 5:1-10	Colossians 1:9-23
		Psalm 119:1-8
		1 John 3:16-24
Hebrews 13:1	Romans 14:1-23	1 John 4:19-21
	Galatians 2:11-14	1 Thessalonians 4:9-12
	Acts 15:36-40	Ephesians 4:25-32
		Matthew 18:15-22
Matthew 5:9	Ephesians 2:11-22	1 Corinthians 1:10-17
	Colossians 3:1-25	Titus 3:1-11
		Philippians 2:1-4
		Acts 2:42-47
		Psalm 133:1-3
Psalm 19:14	1 Peter 3:8-12	James 3:5-18
	James 4:11-12	Ephesians 4:1-7
	John 17:20-26	Matthew 7:1-5
		1 Thessalonians 5:1-23
		Philippians 4:1-11

YOUR STORY...

Carla had never been to "church" at all. As a 24-year-old new mother, Carla understood fatigue, hardship, and anxiety. She was searching for something - needing something - she just didn't know what.

Then a dear friend invited Carla to church. There, she was introduced to The Great Shepherd, The Everlasting Father, The Prince of Peace. This Deliverer's gift of salvation offered hope, Carla learned, if she elected to follow Him. Here was the "something" she had been seeking.

Carla did not dally. Within three months of hearing the gospel, and learning what she must do to become a child of God, Carla and her boyfriend were married, and baptized. *"We wanted to get married before we were baptized. We were both ready to start living a better life,"* Carla said.

Positive role models in her church family encourage her, and she *"is grateful for their influence on her life and the lives of her children,"* Carla said.

While life is still often hard, an inner calm – a peace – now dominates Carla's heart, and all because a friend cared enough to introduce her to the greatest man who ever lived, Jesus Christ.

~Carla, 41

Growing Panes
No. 7-024

WEEK 25
The churches of Christ

DATES

_____ TO _____

Trying to get to Heaven? Stop! Jesus will take you there.

Monday
The Church of Christ

Christ promised to establish what became the universal Church of Christ. As the world-wide Kingdom of God it is composed of all baptized believers, both living and dead. It is organized around Christ as Head with the apostles and prophets as the foundation. It is eternal.

Tuesday
Local Independent churches of Christ

Most of these individual Christians become members of local churches where they assemble together for worship, fellowship and shared work. Local churches are self-governed with elders and deacons and independent of all other churches.

Wednesday
The Work of the Local Congregation

The local church is to do good works. Christians labor and cooperate for each other's good, as well as for the increase and edification of the Church of Christ as individual members of a local church of Christ. Local Christians are *defacto* members of the universal church.

Thursday
Cooperation to the Glory of God

Local churches of Christ are independent of each other regarding all purely local matters. But in all matters of general interest regarding efficiency of the whole body to fulfill the mission for which the church was established, they may and should cooperate with other churches of Christ.

Friday
As the Bride of Christ

The Church of Christ's relationship to Jesus is compared with the relationship of a wife to a husband, as the Bride of Christ. Many comparisons can be made, but the bride's submission is one of the strongest.

INSIDE TRACK	MIDDLE LANES	FAST TRACK
☐ Acts 20:28	☐ Matthew 16:13-20	☐ Acts 2:40-41
	☐ Hebrews 12:18-29	☐ Ephesians 1:22-23.
	☐	☐ Colossians 1:18-19
		☐ Psalm 118:22-23
		☐
☐ Romans 16:16	☐ Ephesians 4:1-18	☐ 1 Timothy 3:14-15
	☐ 1 Corinthians 12:12-31	☐ Titus 1:5
	☐ Romans 16:1-16	☐ Acts 6:1-7
		☐ 1 Peter 5:1-4
		☐
☐ Ephesians 4:11-13	☐ Ephesians 2:1-9	☐ Acts 2:42-47
	☐ Romans 12:3-21	☐ Colossians 3:15-17
	☐ 1 Corinthians 12:7-27	☐ 1 Corinthians 11:17-29
		☐ Acts 4:32-35
		☐ 1 Corinthians 5:9-13
☐ Matthew 28:18-20	☐ Romans 15:23-33	☐ Ephesians 2:19-22
	☐ 2 Corinthians 8:1-15	☐ 2 Corinthians 9:1-5
	☐	☐ Acts 11:1-18
		☐
		☐
☐ Revelation 19:7	☐ Ephesians 5:25-32	☐ 2 Corinthians 11:2
	☐ Revelation 21:1-4	☐ 1 Corinthians 3:16-17
	☐	☐ Revelation 19:1-7
		☐
		☐

YOUR STORY...

"I asked myself, if I had to stand before God today, what would he say to me? I didn't like what I thought he would say."

Larry was unhappy, bored, and regretful. The more he thought about his life, the more he realized he was missing a lot of things — joy, peace, and contentment, to name a few. *"My life just wasn't going well,"* Larry said. Reflecting on past mistakes in his life, Larry longed for serenity, a pardon granting freedom from regret and remorse.

John Klimko, Byron Brown and Kevin Boyd helped Larry understand that through baptism, his past sins would be forgiven and he would have a new life in Jesus Christ, he said.

Larry knew this was the missing link, the answer to his discontent. Larry is paralyzed from the waist down, so logistics posed a tiny bit of an issue. That issue was quickly resolved, however, when permission was granted to use the Graystone Way Rehab Center pool, and these three men were on hand to help Larry in and out of the water. On February 16, 2018, at the age of 65, Larry was baptized.

With the slate wiped clean, Larry is no longer troubled by what God might say to him at judgment. He knows heaven will be his eternal home, and he shares this personal insight: *"Life is precious. Don't waste it like I did for so long. Life is so much more fulfilling with Christ in it."*
~Larry, 65

Growing Panes

No. 7-025

WEEK 26
Confident in "I Believe..."

The mighty oak was a little nut that stood its ground.

INSIDE TRACK	MIDDLE LANES	FAST TRACK

Monday
The Faith

The Word contained in The Book is the only infallible and totally reliable standard of our faith and practice. Timothy was told to preach it and Jude says we are to contend for it. "The faith" is God's scheme of redemption.

- ☐ 2 Corinthians 11:1-4
- ☐ Acts 6:1-7
- ☐ Galatians 1:6-24
- ☐ Jude 1:3-4
- ☐ Revelation 10:1-7
- ☐ 2 Peter 2:4-5
- ☐ Jude 1:6-7
- ☐ 1 John 5:1-5
- ☐ Romans 8:35-39

Tuesday
Belief in the Heart

Our hearts must be full of faith, and our lives faithful as we test our thoughts, our words, our actions by the Divine standard, "the faith." They must be brought up to as near the standard as possible, but not go beyond it.

- ☐ Genesis 1:26
- ☐ Hebrews 11:1-12
- ☐ Matthew 8:5-13
- ☐ Matthew 25:21-28
- ☐ Genesis 1:26-31
- ☐ Genesis 2:4-9
- ☐ Genesis 2:18-24
- ☐ Genesis 3:8-15
- ☐ Hebrews 2:14-15

Wednesday
Faith and Obedience

Such a heart of faith will cause a person to trust Christ and to obey His commandments. Faith and obedience come to represent the life of a disciple. Faith in action then will produce "faithfulness," a fruit of the Spirit.

- ☐ Acts 3:21
- ☐ Romans 1:8-17
- ☐ Galatians 5:22-26
- ☐ Matthew 23:23-24
- ☐ Acts 3:17-23
- ☐ 2 Peter 3:11-13
- ☐ Revelation 21:1-2
- ☐ Isaiah 65:17-19
- ☐ Isaiah 66:22-24

Thursday
Faith in Practice

Faithful Christians *do* what they *say; they practice what they preach.* Every disciple should want to set an example of the believer. By being doers of the Word, we show the world by our faith what a follower of Jesus looks like.

- ☐ 2 Thess. 2:13
- ☐ James 2:1-25
- ☐ Colossians 3:15-17
- ☐ Romans 12:9-20
- ☐ 2 Thessalonians 2:13-17
- ☐ 1 Peter 1:1-2
- ☐ Colossians 1:11-14
- ☐ Hebrews 9:11-15
- ☐ Ephesians 3:1-7

Friday
"This I Believe..."

Currently, the end of our faith is confidence, but when Christ comes again, a crown of life. Disciples should continually confirm that they are in "the faith." Then, remain faithful until death.

- ☐ Romans 11:33
- ☐ 2 Timothy 4:1-8
- ☐ 2 Timothy 3:10-17
- ☐
- ☐ Romans 11:33-36
- ☐ Isaiah 45:18-19
- ☐ Isaiah 55:8-13
- ☐ Job 36:22-33
- ☐ 1 Corinthians 2:1-12

YOUR STORY...

Powerful lessons and soul-stirring singing during the last night of SonQuest reverberated through Jade's 12-year old heart.

A shared love for Christ illuminated the assembly, creating a welcoming, palpable comradery. Jade longed to be a part of this brotherhood of believers.

Jade knew that baptism was required of her, and she was ready to obey. But, Jade wanted to take that salvation step at home, surrounded by family and friends, and she wanted her minister to baptize her. So Jade waited until the Sunday she arrived back home to put Christ on in baptism.

Jade's life has changed in a profound way, she said. She tries to take stock of every word, every action, analyzing them through the lens of Christ's example. *"I try to intentionally let my actions and interactions with others reflect the love of Christ,"* Jade said.

She prays that through those actions and interactions she will *"be able to bring others to Christ,"* and influence them for good, just as she was influenced for good. *"I want to be a light for the rest of the world."*

~Jade, 17

Growing Panes

No. 7-026

"WHO'S PACKING YOUR PARACHUTE?"

Charles Plumb, a U.S. Naval Academy graduate, was a jet pilot in Vietnam. After 75 combat missions, his plane was destroyed by a surface-to-air missile. Plumb ejected and parachuted into enemy hands. He was captured and spent six years in a communist Vietnamese prison. He survived the ordeal and now lectures on lessons learned from that experience.

One day, when Plumb and his wife were sitting in a restaurant, a man at another table came up and said, "You're Plumb! You flew jet fighters in Vietnam from the aircraft carrier Kitty Hawk. You were shot down!"

"How in the world did you know that?" asked Plumb.

"I packed your parachute," the man replied.

Plumb gasped in surprise and gratitude.

The man pumped his hand and said, "I guess it worked!"

Plumb assured him, "It sure did. If your chute hadn't worked, I wouldn't be here today."

Plumb couldn't sleep that night, thinking about that man. Plumb says, "I kept wondering what he might have looked like in a Navy uniform: a white hat, a bib in the back, and bell-bottom trousers. I wonder how many times I might have seen him and not even said 'Good morning,' 'how are you?' or anything because, you see, I was a fighter pilot and he was just a sailor." Plumb thought of the many hours the sailor had spent on a long wooden table in the bowels of the ship, carefully weaving the shrouds and folding the silks of each chute, holding in his hands each time the fate of someone he didn't know.

Now, Plumb asks his audience, "Who's packing your parachute?"

- Author Unknown -

None of us should leave this world through death to face God in judgment without a spiritual parachute that represents our religious beliefs and convictions of faith. What we believe and how we practice our faith is "our parachute" to safety in the world to come. It is critically important "who" packed your 'chute and "how" your parachute is packed! The BRM is designed to encourage the use of the Bible only in "packing your 'chute" for eternity.

WEEK 27
Fortunes and Destiny of the Redeemed
Bonus Victory Lap

DATES

_____ TO _____

Monday
Second Coming of Christ

At the end of time Christ will again return to the earth to execute judgment and to take the redeemed home to be with Him. Every eye will see him when he returns. The final battle with the forces of evil will be fought. Christ and the forces of good will be victorious.

Tuesday
Resurrection from the Dead

The dead will be raised, and those who remain alive will be changed. Our resurrected bodies will be immortal, spiritual bodies. The resurrection of Jesus is evident proof that God will raise us in the last days.

Wednesday
Day of Judgment

In addition to the resurrection, Christ will come to execute judgment. Both good and evil will stand before his judgment throne to be judged by Him. We will be judged according to our works, how we lived our lives on earth. Jesus will be the righteous and merciful judge.

Thursday
Separation from Evil

After the final judgment the Redeemed of the earth will be separated from the evils of Satan. The Devil and his angels will be in torment; whereas, the Redeemed of the earth will be in Heaven. The former will suffer punishment and separation from the face of God.

Friday
Eternal Home in Heaven

Thus will be consummated the eternal Scheme of Redemption with our home in Heaven. It will be like living in a perfect eternal city where all the good things are provided and all the bad things are absent. Heaven is our home of the soul.

INSIDE TRACK	MIDDLE LANES	FAST TRACK
☐ Mark 13:32	☐ John 14:1-4	☐ 2 Peter 3:8-9
	☐ Acts 1:1-11	☐ Matthew 24:4-5
	☐ 2 Thessalonians 2:1-11	☐ Revelation 1:7
		☐ Luke 21:34-36
		☐
☐ 1 Corinthians 15:56-57	☐ 1 Corinthians 15:50-54	☐ Romans 2:5-11
	☐ 1 Thess. 4:13-18	☐ Daniel 7:12-14
	☐	☐ Matthew 24:30-44
		☐
		☐
☐ Acts 17:31	☐ Acts 17:22-34	☐ Romans 1:18-20
	☐ Revelation 20:11-15	☐ Matthew 24:22-27
	☐	☐ Job 34:10-15
		☐ 2 Corinthians 5:1-10
		☐
☐ Matthew 25:41	☐ Matthew 25:31-46	☐ Matthew 7:13-27
	☐ 2 Thessalonians 1:5-12	☐ 2 Timothy 4:1-8
	☐ Luke 16:19-31	☐ 1 Corinthians 9:24-27
		☐
		☐
☐ Matthew 25:34	☐ Revelation 21:1-27	☐ 2 Peter 3:1-18
	☐	☐ 2 Peter 1:3-11
	☐	☐ 1 Corinthians 15:20-28
		☐
		☐

MY "FIRSTS"...

I was excited to be moving to a small town in Southeastern Oklahoma for my *first* full-time preaching job. The small church with fewer than ninety members was also excited because I would be their *first* full-time minister.

Soon after moving in, Jane approached me requesting that I officiate at her upcoming wedding. Jane was the daughter of one of the elders of the church. She had four sibling sisters, which included a set of twins. This marriage ceremony also would be a "*first*" for me, and I agreed to do it.

The wedding was a happy community event. The small clapboard church building was filled to capacity. All the church members and many from the town came. Jane's father was also the high school principal, so dozens of students and teachers filled the pews. Jane and "Bob" were sent away on their honeymoon with all the conclusive trappings of a joyous Oklahoma wedding.

Just a few hours later the call came. There had been a terrible automobile accident. "Bob" was killed.

A few days later I conducted my *first* funeral.

"How do you know what your life will be like tomorrow? Your life is like the morning fog—it's here a little while, then it's gone (James 4:14). "

Tomorrow is not a sure thing!   - grh

Growing Panes

No. 7-027

Test Yourself Quiz

One question is taken from each of the 27 weeks of the race. This is an open book test. Go to the week number (Question #) to check your answers.

1) **Eve ate from the tree in the middle of the garden when:**
   ( ) She saw it was good to eat
   ( ) It was pleasing to the eye
   ( ) To gain wisdom

2) **Noah was saved in the ark because:**
   ( ) He had worked building it
   ( ) He was righteous
   ( ) He took the animals in

3) **Circumcision was:**
   ( ) A sign of the covenant
   ( ) A sign of worship
   ( ) A sign of God's care

4) **Moses told Pharaoh to let the people go:**
   ( ) To be free from slavery
   ( ) To worship God
   ( ) To become a nation of God

5) **Jesus is our:**
   ( ) Sin offering
   ( ) Paschal lamb
   ( ) Deliverer

6) **The Tabernacle was built:**
   ( ) As a memorial to God
   ( ) As a house for God
   ( ) As a house for Levites

7) **The church began on this holy day:**
   ( ) Passover
   ( ) Sabbath Day
   ( ) Pentecost

8) **The "Promised land" refers to:**
   ( ) Canaan
   ( ) Goshen
   ( ) Heaven

9) **Jesus grew up in:**
   ( ) Jerusalem
   ( ) Nazareth
   ( ) Bethlehem

10) **Jesus is the mediator of:**
    ( ) The covenant of Moses
    ( ) The covenant of Israel
    ( ) A new covenant

11) **The "Word" became flesh:**
    ( ) To save sinners
    ( ) To leave us an example
    ( ) To defeat Satan

12) **In the conversion of sinners the Holy Spirit:**
    ( ) Is the Word of God
    ( ) Works through the Word
    ( ) Neither one

13) **The truth of God in NT days was:**
    ( ) Revealed to Apostles
    ( ) Confirmed by miracles
    ( ) Accepted with divine gifts

14) **The church of Christ was to be established on:**
    ( ) Water Baptism
    ( ) Good Confession
    ( ) Liberal Giving

15) **All spiritual blessings are:**
    ( ) In Christ
    ( ) In the Holy Spirit
    ( ) In heaven

16) **"Preachers" are "Pastors":**
    ( ) Yes
    ( ) No
    ( ) Maybe

17) **As a preacher, Timothy was told to:**
    ( ) Preach the Word
    ( ) Preach his convictions
    ( ) Preach what works

18) **Singing is an act of worship involving the strings of the heart.**
    ( ) True
    ( ) False

19) **The early Church met for congregational worship on:**
    ( ) Sabbath (Saturday)
    ( ) Lord's Day (Sunday)
    ( ) Any day of the week

20) **Acceptable observance of the Lord's Supper requires:**
    ( ) A sinless life
    ( ) Self-examination
    ( ) A common meal also

21) **The world will know that we are His disciples by our love:**
    ( ) True
    ( ) False

22) **Jesus said we serve Him:**
    ( ) By serving brothers and sisters
    ( ) By serving ourselves
    ( ) By being in the church

23) **Which of these is "the greatest"?**
    ( ) Faith
    ( ) Hope
    ( ) Love

24) **Jesus as the Prince of Peace was proclaimed to:**
    ( ) Kings of the earth
    ( ) Shepherds in the field
    ( ) Joseph and Mary

25) **Disciples are created in the church of Christ for:**
    ( ) Worship
    ( ) Good Works
    ( ) Edification of others

26) **Jude says Christians are to "contend for the faith" once delivered...**
    ( ) True
    ( ) False

27) **In the last day our judge will be:**
    ( ) God, the Father
    ( ) God, the Son
    ( ) God, the Holy Spirit

Test yourselves and find out if you really are true to your faith. If you pass the test, you will discover that Christ is living in you. But if Christ isn't living in you, you have failed.

2 Corinthians 13:5
Contemporary English Version

www.ingramcontent.com/pod-product-compliance
Lightning Source LLC
Chambersburg PA
CBHW041220040426

42443CB00002B/29